"In this powerful book, Kathy DeGraw arms you with spiritual weapons and revelatory strategies that will better equip, train and prepare you in spiritual warfare. I highly recommend this work, written with such a prophetic edge and apostolic insight that reveals the many unseen fortresses keeping people shackled to their past and locked out of their future. You will learn how the enemy systematically uses trauma, pain, rejection, abuse, fear and addiction—just to name a few—as building blocks to create strongholds, fortifications and walls against your future with God. *Unshackled* is like a wrecking ball in the hands of the reader to break past every invisible barrier. This is a must-read!"

Dr. Naim Collins, president, Naim Collins Ministries;
author, *Realms of the Prophetic*

"Soul wounds, generational curses, fear and emotional ailments . . . In this broken world, we're all in need of inner healing. The Lord has gifted Kathy DeGraw in profound ways and shown her practical steps everyone can take to receive deliverance. This powerful and anointed book will show you how to receive the deliverance and inner healing you need to live abundantly and free of fear, and help you discover God's prophetic destiny for your life."

Troy Anderson, Pulitzer Prize–nominated journalist;
bestselling author; former executive editor, *Charisma*

"We need a voice to equip us in spiritual warfare in these evil days to keep us from the slithering grip of the evil one. Apostle Kathy DeGraw is a voice that cannot and will not be silent, but will arise and bring deliverance, shutting down the twisted world of darkness and terror. Kathy DeGraw has been used and is still being used strategically by God to bring deliverance, healing and strong freedom for God's people. This is the anointed blueprint I recommend to anyone who is looking to reach another level in Christ Jesus. Surely the author's mind and hands have been inspired by Holy Spirit to write such a masterpiece."

Apostle Luis Lopez Jr., D.Div., author, *The Counterfeit Christian*;
Luis Lopez Media Ministries International

"In *Unshackled*, Kathy DeGraw brings to light the dark strategies of hell that keep many in bondage. I can literally and spiritually see the chains falling off people as they read it! If you desire to break free of demonic shackles that have limited you for years, this is the book for you.

"DeGraw identifies ten of the most potent strongholds of the enemy and supplies the tools to dismantle them. I love the way Kathy shares personal experiences in order to expound on biblical principles.

"I am impressed by the oil (anointing) that is on Kathy's book. I believe the residue will remain long after the reader has finished it. The word *anointing* also means 'effectiveness.' DeGraw has effectively communicated concepts that will assist the average believer in gaining an advantage over Satan. This is a must-have for your library. If you don't purchase this book, you'll be missing a much-needed weapon to add to your deliverance war chest."

Dr. John Veal, author, *Supernaturally Delivered*
and *Supernaturally Prophetic*

"Recognizing the need for deliverance in other people seems effortless; the true test of spiritual maturity is applying that very same diligence to ourselves. Apostle Kathy DeGraw's *Unshackled* contains instructions on self-deliverance, on recognizing issues that expose the need for deliverance and, most importantly, on how to be liberated by God through His Holy Word. Apostle DeGraw's books have always been spiritually concise, thought-provoking, revelatory and Spirit-filled. Spiritual nuggets have been released for all who desire to be set free in heart, mind, body and spirit. I am convinced that whosoever reads this book will be set free from the *inside out*!"

Pastor Tomeka Bratcher, My Father's House
Christian Discipleship Ministries

"Apostle Kathy DeGraw has written a practical and encouraging manual on healing and deliverance. She walks you through steps to identify soul wounds, fear, rejection and other forms of debilitating trauma, and she gives you the tools through knowing Jesus and the power of His Word that will bring you the healing and deliverance you need. She also shares personal stories of her own deliverance and healing, which shows the power of the Gospel over her own life. If you want to learn to have the victory through knowing who you are in Christ to overcome difficult areas in your life, this resource is for you!"

Dr. Candice Smithyman, founder, Dream Mentors International;
host, *Glory Road TV Show*

UNSHACKLED

UNSHACKLED

BREAKING THE STRONGHOLDS *of* YOUR PAST
TO RECEIVE
COMPLETE DELIVERANCE

KATHY DeGRAW

Chosen
a division of Baker Publishing Group
Minneapolis, Minnesota

© 2020 by Kathy DeGraw

Published by Chosen Books
11400 Hampshire Avenue South
Bloomington, Minnesota 55438
www.chosenbooks.com

Chosen Books is a division of
Baker Publishing Group, Grand Rapids, Michigan

Printed in the United States of America

Library of Congress Cataloging-in-Publication Data
Names: DeGraw, Kathy, author.
Title: Unshackled : breaking the strongholds of your past to receive complete deliverance / Kathy DeGraw.
Description: Minneapolis, Minnesota : Chosen Books, [2020]
Identifiers: LCCN 2019059825 | ISBN 9780800799977 (trade paperback) | ISBN 9781493426539 (ebook)
Subjects: LCSH: Spiritual healing—Christianity. | Repentance—Christianity. | Forgiveness—Religious aspects. | Spiritual warfare.
Classification: LCC BT732.5 .D454 2020 | DDC 248.8/6—dc23
LC record available at https://lccn.loc.gov/2019059825

In some of the author's stories, names and identifying details have been changed to protect their privacy.

Cover design by LOOK Design Studio

20 21 22 23 24 25 26   7 6 5 4 3 2 1

Pamela Kamstra—
Thank you for your faithful service to the Kingdom and to me for ten years. A dedication isn't long enough to mention everything you have done for me and all the sentiments I have for you. You became the ultimate prayer warrior who assisted me in setting thousands of people free and who made sure my backside was covered against demonic attacks. My Pammy girl, I'll miss traveling the world with you!

CONTENTS

1. What Is Inner Healing?   23

   Soul wounds affect each of us and leave places in our lives that need healing from hurt, offenses and abuses. Jesus didn't only purchase salvation at the cross. He also purchased our healing and deliverance, empowering us to live in victory and abundant life.

2. Keys of Freedom: Repentance and Forgiveness   29

   Repentance and forgiveness are foundational keys to walking successfully as Christians and breaking spiritual and emotional strongholds in our lives.

3. Fear   47

   Fear is tormenting and traumatizing. Behind emotional ailments, we can discover something we fear. Behind every fear is a lie we believe. Meditating on the Scriptures and mind renewal are key elements

us seek refuge in an addiction instead of in God is crucial to removing not only these bad habits, but also demonic strongholds in our lives. Root out once and for all the deep strongholds of addiction so that you find more than a temporary cycle of freedom; you find a permanent freedom that lasts forever.

FOREWORD

Unshackled helps you examine your life to find areas of brokenness, and then guides you through self-deliverance using the powerful antidote of spiritual warfare and inner healing. As an apostolic leader and prophetic healing expert, Kathy DeGraw leads readers to discover how to overcome Satan's insidious tactics. She will clearly show you necessary warfare strategies and techniques available in your full weaponry through Christ to clean house by arresting the strongman that has been occupying those places in your spiritual house.

Unshackled is for every Spirit-filled believer and leadership team who is ready to break ancient strongholds of the past while receiving supernatural wholeness in every area of our lives. Second Corinthians 10:4 (MEV) says, "For the weapons of our warfare are not carnal, but mighty through God to the pulling down of strong holds." This exceptional literary work contains an arsenal of content weaponry that will teach all believers how to identify, classify, discern and destroy the ten most subtle unseen trespassers and strongholds violating our lives.

I highly endorse the pages of this groundbreaking book. It carries a strong tangible anointing of freedom in God's delivering power. After reading this deliverance handbook, you will go from being shackled in fear, doubt, oppression, debt, torment and unbelief to unshackled in every area, with the power of God's glory to experience total liberty, soul healing, cleansing and divine blessings.

Dr. Hakeem Collins, Champions International;
author, *Heaven Declares, 10 Prayer Secrets*

OPENING PROPHETIC WORD

Note: The Lord spoke to me years ago about starting and ending my books with a prophetic word. Through prophetic words, the Lord reveals to someone what He wants to release to people. Such a word should always be consistent with Scripture, and as it is released, it is in the first person, as though God were speaking it Himself. The following word is what I heard through prayer that God wants to say to you, the reader, as you begin this book.

Joy, abundant joy, is what I desire for you. You have been through hardships; the pain you suffered I have felt. But I know the joy that also comes in the morning and the mourning. You've lost your joy because you've forgotten how to grieve and how to heal. My Son, Jesus, purchased your healing and deliverance, and now it is time to walk in the freedom we both long for you to have.

You will have exceedingly more joy than you can imagine. The enemy has stifled your joy; now it is time to pick yourself up and move along. We are going to travel this road together, toward your freedom, and no weapon formed against you will prosper. No more blockages will hinder your freedom. You are on a new journey now. One I will walk with you. I am here for you, and with your help to push through to your breakthrough, you will receive exceedingly abundant joy!

HOW TO USE THIS BOOK

I designed this book as a tool that will help you do self-deliverance. It will educate you on this topic, and on how an emotional ailment or trauma can become a spiritual stronghold in your life. It will show you the areas where you need to find freedom and how to walk out your deliverance so that you get free and stay free.

Spiritual Self-Assessment

I talk in chapter 1 about what inner healing is and how to determine if you need it. Then starting in chapter 2, you will find a seven-statement spiritual assessment to take before you read each chapter. Rate each of the seven statements on a scale of 1 to 10 as it applies to you, with 1 being "this is not very applicable to me" and 10 being "I am off the charts in this area." The score you give yourself will show to what degree you feel you need freedom in that area. In fact, it is good to keep in mind that we all need more freedom in most areas.

Insights from Each Chapter

As you read each chapter, take time to reflect on the content I share. It is content based on my years of experience helping people find freedom in their lives from these different strongholds I address. Proceed through the chapters slowly, or at whatever pace the Holy Spirit leads you, in order to gain maximum impact from this book and be able to work yourself through deliverance and receive the full freedom you desire.

Walking Out Your Deliverance

At the end of each chapter, you will find practical applications in how to walk out your deliverance. These include a list of powerful Scriptures to look up on each topic, a prayer of repentance and forgiveness, a list of spirits often associated with each topic so you can discern and cast them out, a prayer of activation to fill the void they leave behind with something better, and both faith declarations and spiritual warfare declarations to speak out as often as needed to maintain your freedom. Let's look briefly at how to use each of these applications.

Scriptures on . . . (each topic)

Fill yourself up with Scripture. In the "Scriptures on . . ." sections, I list Scriptures you can lean on that are the opposite of whatever you cast out. They will encourage you in your deliverance. To find even more Scriptures, you can do a word search in your Bible or a Bible app of the opposite of whatever you cast out. An example would be to find and read Scriptures on faith if you cast out fear.

Prayer of Repentance and Forgiveness

I encourage you to speak the repentance and forgiveness prayers in each chapter aloud. Allow your emotions to arise, and feel the repentance and forgiveness you are releasing. If you cannot forgive yourself or others, go back to chapter 2, the forgiveness chapter, and try those exercises again. Revisit that chapter as often as necessary to work through how to forgive people. It is important to speak out forgiving yourself and others, since sometimes if we cannot do that or if the words won't come out, our mind cannot then comprehend forgiving, or demons will attempt to block that forgiveness from coming forth.

As you speak out, you are taking authority over the demonic realm and releasing the offender of the offense. Keep trying until you successfully speak out the forgiveness and start to feel the correlating emotion of forgiveness in your heart. While forgiveness is not a feeling (and I talk about that later), if you keep speaking it out even when it is hard to do, you will start to feel a release and a peace within your heart that you really have forgiven yourself or someone else. It is okay if you occasionally have to come back and forgive a person (or yourself) again. Simply acknowledge that you are not there yet. Keep the book in front of you, and keep coming back and working through the forgiveness exercises.

Spirits to Discern and Cast Out

Once we have repented of situations that apply to us and have offered forgiveness, we have removed the legal rights of demonic entities to attack us in those areas. When we receive inner healing, we also need to cast out the spirits, as Jesus did. When we don't cast out the spirits, we simply mask the problems for a little while, but the enemy will still attack us in spiritual warfare. At the end of each chapter, I list which spirits can be attached to certain emotional ailments. You can either cast out all the spirits listed, or you can ask the Holy Spirit for discernment on which specific spirits to cast out. When casting out spirits, say, "Spirit of _____ (insert spirit name), I command you to go, in Jesus' name."

You may or may not feel something as a spirit leaves. In my book *Discerning and Destroying the Works of Satan* (Destiny Image, 2018), I provide three different lists of demonic manifestations.

I recommend casting out a demon and repeating the commanding sentence until you feel peace, a spiritual shift or a physical manifestation. If you feel a tightening in your chest or feel as if a demon is resisting leaving, say out loud, "I break agreement with _____ (insert spirit's name), and I command you to get out of me, in Jesus' name."

One of the reasons people don't receive complete inner healing is because they don't cast out the demonic spirit associated with their trauma or healing issue. Deliverance is obtained in its fullness when we practice the deliverance model Jesus exuded from His ministry. When we search the Scriptures, we see that He cast the spirits out. Reflect on previous deliverance you have received. Have those who ministered to you said, "Spirit of _____ (the emotional or spirit name), I cast you out, in Jesus' name"? We must speak audibly, take authority and cast the demons out.

How can a demon infiltrate a Christian who is filled with the Holy Spirit? We are a three-part being: spirit, soul and physical body. Our spirit, where the Holy Spirit resides, cannot be infiltrated by a demon. A demon cannot possess a Christian. It can, however, oppress a Christian. It can oppress and infiltrate our soul, which is our mind, will and emotions. And it can infiltrate our physical body, causing physical infirmities.

As you go through each list of associated spirits and say "spirit of _____ (insert name), go, in Jesus' name," trust that the spirits will leave. Have faith and move forward not in legalism, but in the discernment of the Lord that He will lead and guide you through the deliverance process. Ultimately remember, too, that not everything is demonic.

Prayer of Activation

After we have cast demonic spirits out, we need to fill up that empty space left behind. The Bible instructs us to fill up the void so the spirits don't come back seven times worse (see Luke 11:24–26). Read the activation prayer in each chapter from a position of believing and receiving that God will impart to you what you are praying for, and that you are going to have what you say.

It is equally important in the days, weeks and months following your deliverance that you fill up spiritually through prayer, worship and Bible study. Keep allowing the Holy Spirit to speak to you, and work on getting into a close relationship with God the Father, Jesus our Lord, and the Holy Spirit. You can also view some of my videos online for additional teaching and help growing in your walk with the Lord (visit YouTube @Kathy DeGraw).

Expect spiritual warfare attacks in the season after you receive deliverance. The enemy is not going to want you free, but by filling up and getting close to the Lord, you can combat these attacks. I have also written some other books that can assist you in knowing how to combat spiritual warfare through specific declarative prayers: *Warfare Declarations* (CreateSpace, 2017) and *Prophetic Proclamations* (K Publishing, 2019).

Declarations to Speak Out

Speak out the declarations at the very end of each chapter audibly. Bookmark the declaration pages in the book and come back to them often to assist you in renewing your mind, transforming your heart and increasing your faith. Speak out the *Faith Declarations* with authority, believing that you will receive them. Speak them out from a position of *I have these*, not *I'm trying to obtain these*. Christ has already purchased our freedom on the cross. Now we have to receive it!

The *Spiritual Warfare Declarations* will move you past declaring in faith, to taking up your authority to bind and restrict the enemy and counteract future attacks. As you read these declarations, stand up, if you are able. Put your entire self into speaking out and releasing these into the spiritual atmosphere. Engage your physical body, your emotions and your spirit being. Take your God-given authority to declare these and annihilate the enemy. Expect further deliverance to manifest as you speak the spiritual warfare declarations out audibly. They are not to be read silently, but are to be spoken out loud. Use them if you feel spiritual warfare and attack. Use them if you have opened a door to sin or demonic infiltration and need to close it. Use them if you are being plagued with fatigue or defeat. These are important weapons in a powerful arsenal that you can use to combat the attacks of the enemy. Declare them out loud again and again. Keep at it until you feel victory, release and freedom!

Part 1

FINDING FREEDOM THROUGH INNER HEALING AND DELIVERANCE

CHAPTER 1

WHAT IS INNER HEALING?

I didn't grow up knowing about healing ministry. I had been to different denominational churches as a young adult, and I had never even heard the term mentioned. I didn't know I needed healing. I just knew there were some things about myself that I didn't like very much. I didn't like being scared of walking in the dark, driving on bridges over water and driving in unknown places. I didn't like it that when I got mad, I would yell and scream from the pit of my gut and at the top of my lungs. I knew there were things I needed to purge, but I didn't know how to purge them, or even that I could be free of them. I didn't realize that in the places in my soul where I needed healing, evil spirits were affecting me.

My husband, Ron, was pastoring a church when I felt a stirring inside me that there must be more to Christianity than what I was experiencing. I was eager for more of the Lord, and when I started reading some books in my search, I stumbled on one about the baptism of the Holy Spirit. Reading that, I knew I desired to have the fullness of the Holy Spirit residing inside me!

One day my husband said, "We're going to be in healing and deliverance ministry."

I said, "No, I'm going into *healing* ministry (praying to heal the sick), and you're going into *deliverance* ministry (casting out demons)."

I hardly knew anything about deliverance except that we were currently in a spiritual battle within our church. God had plans for us that were different than my plans, however. Today I am a deliverance minister, casting out demons and teaching people to conquer the powers of darkness, while my husband focuses on physical healing and praying for the sick.

I began spending hours every day with the Lord. Over two years I sought Him, prayed, worshiped, studied my Bible and went to church a lot. I wanted everything He had for me. It was during that season that I began to receive conviction about the things that needed to change in my life. In my prayer time, I would receive deliverance from the Lord from ungodly behavioral patterns, generational curses and emotional ailments.

The Lord brought forth inner healing, deliverance and instruction during those two years I spent diligently seeking Him. Inner healing is an important part of deliverance ministry. Inner healing is receiving the emotional healing we need and working ourselves through our emotions and the forgiveness process. Deliverance is casting out the correlating demonic spirit that could have infiltrated our souls as a result of holding onto our affliction for so long.

We must be cleansed in our souls of emotional wounds, traumas and demonic oppression. When we seek inner healing and don't cast out the correlating demonic spirit, we are simply masking our issue temporarily. We may experience some immediate relief, but when another extreme instance of what troubles us manifests, we find ourselves in just as much bondage, or more, than we previously experienced. If not cast out, an oppressive spirit associated with our situation lies dormant and inactive, until another trauma comes up and triggers it. When we receive inner healing but don't cast out the spirits, as Jesus did, the problem can therefore rise again.

Broken Hearts Can Heal

When we have soul wounds, part of our heart feels broken with hurt, disappointment and loneliness. Jesus had compassion on the brokenhearted. Psalm 147:3 (MEV) says, "He heals the broken in heart, and binds up their wounds." Psalm 34:18 (MEV) continues this theme: "The LORD is near to the broken-hearted, and saves the contrite of spirit."

When we come to Jesus for healing, He will do what His Word says. He is passionate to heal the afflicted and repentant. When He died on the cross, it was not just for our salvation. The Hebrew root of the word *salvation* is *yesha*, which is the basis for Yeshua, the Hebrew name of Jesus. This word signifies deliverance or rescue from anything that binds or restricts. Jesus died for the inner healing and deliverance you need.

One of the reasons Jesus went to the cross was to heal us emotionally. Isaiah instructs us, "Surely He has borne our griefs and carried our sorrows; yet we esteemed Him stricken, smitten by God, and afflicted" (Isaiah 53:4). Jesus took the weight of our grief and sorrows on Himself so we could live in victory. He took our emotional ailments to the cross so we don't have to carry them. He carried them for us. When we release our wounds to Jesus, we can live in the victory of the accomplished work of the cross.

Inner healing goes into the deep part of our soul wounds. It does not mean we have to relive a negative experience such as rape, abortion or violence against us. It means we need to allow the Holy Spirit to come in and "Create in me a clean heart" (Psalm 51:10). A clean heart offers forgiveness and exudes love. Having a clean heart is making sure our heart is not hurting. It is allowing Him to come into all the places in our soul (our mind, will and emotions) to make sure they are lining up to God's Word and God's will for our lives.

God does not desire us to live in hurt, fear or rejection. He sent His Son, Jesus, to give us abundant life (see John 10:10). To live abundantly, we need to release through the process of inner healing the situations and people who have hurt us. Inner healing is a process. It is not instantaneous. When we have hung onto hurts for thirty, forty or even sixty years, we cannot expect them to go away overnight. This book will lead you through the process of emotional healing and demonic deliverance so that you can live the abundant life Jesus came to give you.

How Inner Healing Assists Us

Inner healing is looking back at your past in order to move forward. It is not putting yourself through past hurts again. It is exploring what is holding you back from receiving the fullness of God in your life and living in complete victory. It is going back into your past and closing the doors to the enemy, forgiving people who have hurt you and releasing the negative emotions you may still be hanging onto. It is walking through the emotional hurts and wounds that have created trauma in your life.

Are you still struggling with emotional issues you have tried to overcome, such as anger, fear, rejection or unworthiness? Inner healing can assist you in obtaining freedom in areas where you feel stuck and have not been able to experience a breakthrough. Have you ever wondered, *Why am I the way I am? Why do I act this way?* Often, you may look back and think, *That was out of character for me.* You can find freedom from negative behavioral patterns, habits and thoughts when you know what may be causing the problem.

I have taken my experience of ministering inner healing and deliverance to thousands of people and have put what I learned into the pages of this book to help set you free. I have discovered what the entry points are for the demonic and why people have negative experiences that become strongholds. As you read these pages, you will discover the answer to your questions about why you are the way you are. But even more so, I will lead you through the healing process and the process of changing your mindset. Although emotional issues can exist on their own, often the battlefield is in the mind. Along with inner healing, it is important to renew your mind with the Word of God, and it is also important to make positive confessions and proclamations to walk out your deliverance.

The process of inner healing can reveal and release feelings that have been stuffed or hidden inside our souls. Going through emotional or physical trauma can cause us not to want to deal with the reality of a situation. We can shove the associated feelings aside, pretend they don't exist or stuff them so far down deep that we truly forget about them. As we seek out healing, however, the Holy Spirit starts to reveal those things that are hidden.

Our hidden soul wounds project who we are today. I remember a time in my life when the Holy Spirit was revealing to me something I had forgotten about in my past. After He gently led me through the revelation of what had happened, I felt transformed. Where I had been too serious, I now found myself in joy. Where I had not known how to have fun, I now found myself being playful and learning to enjoy life. He even led me to visit a Build-A-Bear Workshop, stuff a bear, jump up and down and twirl around, and kiss the heart that goes inside the bear, just as children do when they build a bear! It was all part of my deliverance process. I would not trade it for anything. Discovering what was inside me was a temporary process that led to everlasting joy and satisfaction in life. My inner wounds had been affecting who I was, even though I did not realize it until I was healed.

We need to be careful when looking back in order to move forward, so that we don't get stuck in the past. We do not want to get caught up in the emotions or trauma of the past. We need to recognize or acknowledge what happened, offer forgiveness to the person, forgive ourselves and move forward so that we can remove the emotional bondage that holds us captive.

Forty years after leaving Egypt, Moses had to go back to his past. He did not want to go back there, but he did. What happened in the end? The people were delivered! It was not just about Moses' freedom and his equipping or obedience as a leader. It was about freeing an entire nation! It is the same with us. When we go back into our past, we can free more than just ourselves; we can also free other people through the knowledge we gain and the experiences we have gone through that led to our healing. Isn't it worth looking back if we can assist other people in obtaining the freedom that they so desperately long for?

Determining If You Need Healing

Deliverance manifests when we work through generational curses, soul ties and word curses. We need healing from the way we were raised, things that were said to us and hurts we took in. We need healing from words we said ourselves and the way we treated people. We need healing from how we think about ourselves and from what was spoken over us that did not edify, exhort, encourage or build us up. It is important, therefore, to determine if we need healing from the past. Here are three questions to ask yourself to see whether or not you may need healing from your past:

- Do you still think about a certain situation and have emotions or tears come forth over it?
- When you hear the name of a person, does it remind you of someone with a similar name who hurt you, spoke negative words against you or betrayed you?
- When you remember or reference a past situation, do you get angry, hurt or offended again?

The true test of deliverance is this: If you truly are healed of something in your past, then it will not cause a negative emotional reaction when you discuss it in the present. My goal in the following chapters is to assist you in receiving the healing you need, so you can proceed in joy and peace to release those things you have been hanging onto.

Jesus came so we could live victoriously and have the fullness of God manifesting inside us. If we are not experiencing the fruits of the Spirit daily, then there are probably places of healing that need to manifest in our life. Seek the Holy Spirit, as I did. Pray! Call out for conviction, instruction and revelation, and then walk in the freedom He releases to you. I pray the Father's blessings on you as you start this endeavor.

CHAPTER 2

KEYS OF FREEDOM: REPENTANCE AND FORGIVENESS

Self-Assessment—Spirit of Offense

On a scale of 1 to 10, rate each statement below.

1. I am holding onto bitterness, resentment and unforgiveness toward a person, or about a situation.
2. I am presently finding it hard to move past an instance of betrayal, rejection or offense.
3. I have tried to forgive, but I find myself having to forgive again because I haven't let go of the situation.
4. I am hanging onto hurt instead of releasing it.
5. I often feel as though others are against me and don't value me.
6. I am often sick, manifesting stress-related symptoms, or I have a generational ailment such as high blood pressure, high cholesterol or diabetes.
7. Emotions still arise within me when I think about or speak of a situation that caused me hurt.

Through some challenging situations, my husband and I learned the power of forgiveness early on in ministry. Sometimes, even when we did not feel as if we had done anything wrong, we would still do all we could to bring forth peace in a situation by extending an apology and asking forgiveness. On more than one occasion, that effort on our part of going the extra mile changed an uncomfortable situation for the better.

Jesus also extended forgiveness: "Then Jesus said, 'Father, forgive them, for they do not know what they do.' And they divided His garments and cast lots" (Luke 23:34). You could not ask for a better example of forgiveness than Jesus calling out from the cross as He was being crucified, "*Father, forgive them.*" He had taken that long walk on the way to the cross, He had been whipped and beaten, and He was in torturous pain, dying the worst death imaginable. Yet in all His suffering, He was the perfect example of forgiveness.

Defining Forgiveness

In the Greek, the word *forgive* means, "To release, to hurl away, and to free yourself."[1] That is what forgiveness is, freeing yourself. Often, the person you are holding unforgiveness toward doesn't even know it. The person you are upset with is not the one being held in bondage by your feelings; you are. Moving toward forgiveness releases us from the bitterness and resentment that caused our feelings of offense and hurt.

How do we do something like forgive someone, which is so against our nature? We do it by following Jesus' example. It was Jesus who took the first step and forgave us all our sins. The Father

1. *Vine's Complete Expository Dictionary of New Testament Words*, s.v. "Forgive," *Strong's* number G863, Blue Letter Bible online, https://www.blueletter bible.org/search/Dictionary/viewTopic.cfm?topic=VT0001113.

sent His one and only Son, Jesus Christ, to take our punishment and die a criminal's death on the cross. Jesus went to hell and back for us. His example should lead us to the ultimate example of offering forgiveness. God takes the initiative and forgives us. Only through Christ's sacrifice and example on the cross can we learn to forgive.

In our flesh, we don't always want to forgive, but we have the empowerment from God to do so:

- We have the provision and example of Jesus Christ.
- We can have the indwelling presence of the Holy Spirit.
- We have the guidance of God's Word.
- We have the power of prayer at our disposal.

Forgiveness Is Not a Feeling

Forgiveness is a conscious decision to wipe the slate clean of all judgment, to give up all resentment, to release the offender from the debt of his or her act and to personally accept the price of reconciliation. God has forgiven us; therefore, we cannot withhold forgiveness from others. Jesus said, "Your heavenly Father will forgive you if you forgive those who sin against you; but if you refuse to forgive them, He will not forgive you" (Matthew 6:14 TLB).

Forgiveness is not a feeling. If you wait until you feel like forgiving, you may never forgive. When you forgive, you are accepting what Jesus did at the cross. Even though what you believe the person did was wrong and you may never receive an apology from him or her, you are choosing to forgive that person based on what Jesus did and not on how you feel. Forgiveness is a two-step process. First, we make a conscious decision to forgive the person in our mind because it is the right thing to do, based on the finished work of the cross. Second, we need to pray and ask Jesus to align our heart to feel the forgiveness we just offered.

Forgiveness does not mean pretending the offense never happened, condoning the wrong or demanding that the offender change

31

his or her behavior. It does not mean you have to put yourself back into a relationship with that person. It is acknowledging that you are not going to allow an offense to hold you in bondage anymore. Forgiveness means not arguing it out anymore, but choosing to release it instead. Forgiveness is not the same as forgetting. You can completely forgive someone and still remember the offense. When you offer forgiveness, however, the hurt won't be so intense, and the memory will fade over time because it is no longer consuming you.

Forgiveness is an expression of love, and love takes the initiative to forgive, even if the offender has not asked for forgiveness. Forgiveness is difficult. It goes against our human nature. We can find the power to forgive through Christ, and we use that power through the indwelling presence of the Holy Spirit. When we feel as if we cannot forgive, that is when we have to rely on the Holy Spirit within us to assist us in the process.

We can block forgiveness from manifesting in our life. When we have been hurt, we can justify why we should not forgive. We get our flesh, stubbornness and emotions involved and hold back the forgiveness that we should extend. The Bible instructs us to take on Christ's character and walk in the Spirit. We must not allow roadblocks or rationalizations to rise and stop us.

Roadblocks to Forgiveness

Self-condemnation is a roadblock to forgiveness. Our mind can be our greatest obstacle in releasing forgiveness, whether to another person or to ourselves. We get stuck on an instance and cannot get past the situation. We get caught up in a trap of punishing ourselves for the wrong we have done, and we feel bad about what we did. We feel that since no one has extended to us the grace we deserve, how can we extend it to others or ourselves?

We are all sinners in need of God's forgiveness. Forgiveness is not automatic. To be free of a problem, we must first recognize that we have the problem. We have to acknowledge our need to forgive ourselves and others before we can begin to heal. It comes through the blood of Jesus; every person alive has the opportunity to receive forgiveness.

Unforgiveness left unconfessed and unhealed can lead to bitterness, resentment and offense. When we allow it to build, it can become a hindrance to our spiritual walk, emotions and health. Renewing our mind and overcoming blockages will assist us in preventing the enemy from having a foothold in our life.

Our thoughts and spiritual strongholds can get in the way when we attempt to forgive. Here are some reasons we may not be ready to release forgiveness:

- We feel entitlement.
- We can't get past the anger.
- We expect to be hurt again.
- We feel self-pity or have a victim mentality.
- We are getting attention (the hurt gives us something to talk about).
- We let pride get in the way.

Rationalizations against Forgiveness

In our minds, we justify the reasons we should not forgive. We tell ourselves things like these:

- *But what if they don't even see how badly they've hurt me?*
- *I'm afraid if I forgive, I'll only get hurt again.*
- *If I forgive them, they'll only go on hurting others.*
- *What they did to me was unfair; they should be punished.*

When God forgives, He no longer holds our sins against us. We don't have the right to hold others' sins against them. Jesus wants us to forgive each other an infinite number of times, not just when we feel like it: "Then Peter came to Him and said, "Lord, how often shall my brother sin against me, and I forgive him? Up to seven times?" Jesus said to him, "I do not say to you, up to seven times, but up to seventy times seven" (Matthew 18:21–22). By an act of our will, we must put away resentment and the desire to punish a person who has wronged us.

Forgiveness does not require denying your pain, hurt or anger. It may take time for the wound to heal, even though you forgive the person who offended you. Forgiveness does not always mean instant and full reconciliation. When you forgive, it can take time and effort by both parties to rebuild trust. Forgiveness does not mean you put yourself in a relationship with the person again; it is best to seek the Holy Spirit for the direction, if any, He would have you take in restoring such a relationship.

If you are struggling to release forgiveness, rely on the Holy Spirit within you to help. I like to tell people if you cannot do it in your own strength, then do it in His strength. We have His power to forgive.

Offense

Forgiveness issues left undealt with will lead to offense, and offense is a stronghold. As we allow unforgiveness to build in our lives, we can experience becoming prideful, rebellious and controlling. These emotional issues and spiritual strongholds develop a spirit of offense in our lives. Offense manifests these ways: *Everyone else is wrong, and I am right. No one ever gives me a chance. They are out to get me.*

A spirit of offense has a defeated mentality, but also takes a very strong stance. People are adamant that they are not wrong. Offense is at the root of people continually leaving their churches, divorcing their spouses and quitting their jobs. Offense is a strongman that will manifest difficulty in every relationship, but an offended person will seldom see that he or she is the problem.

You have to look at the common factor in all your challenges—you. Everyone else and every situation are not the problem. You are the common factor and are most often the problem. The challenge is that with offense, we don't self-examine. Instead, we blame everyone else. When we seek healing, then we will notice that the situations around us are changing because we have changed.

Trust in God and Extend Love

When we lean on the Holy Spirit and rely on His strength within us, and when we spend time in the presence of God, we can extend forgiveness. Partnering with the Spirit and putting our trust in Him, not in man, allows us to release what Jesus purchased for us.

People are not perfect. We need to put our trust in God, not in man. I tell people, "Don't trust me; trust the God within me." Unfortunately, no matter how hard we try, we will fail people in their eyes, and people will fail us. Extending love and forgiveness therefore takes practice. It can require repeated effort, and we may need to do it daily. People will hurt and disappoint us, but the Bible says of faith, hope and love that "the greatest of these is love" (1 Corinthians 13:13). It also says "God is love" (1 John 4:8). We need to be love. Extending love can be an effort in the natural, until we are overflowing with God's supernatural love. The more we forgive and extend God's love, the easier it will become.

Forgiveness also means asking to be forgiven. It helps us realize when we may have been the person who hurt someone else. My mother-in-law was a prime example of being proactive about offering an apology and being a peacemaker. Once when my children were young, she came over for dinner. She insisted they eat their green beans, which I did not make them eat. The next day, she called and apologized to me just in case she had upset me by insisting they eat their green beans. I was not offended in the least.

Being a peacemaker is knowing when we have violated someone else's expectations of us. Seeking forgiveness is searching our heart to acknowledge the Holy Spirit's conviction that we should apologize to a person we have offended. I have learned over the years that it does not matter who is right or wrong. We need to be the person to go and ask for forgiveness. In God's Word, He tells us His heart toward us making amends with people:

> Therefore if you bring your gift to the altar, and there remember that your brother has something against you, leave your gift there before the altar, and go your way. First be reconciled to your brother, and then come and offer your gift. Agree with your adversary quickly, while you are on the way with him, lest your adversary deliver you to the judge, the judge hand you over to the officer, and you be thrown into prison.
>
> Matthew 5:23–25

The Power of Repentance

The Bible makes it clear that there are some conditions we must meet to obtain God's forgiveness. One step in receiving forgiveness is to turn from our ungodly ways and change them. We may struggle with a certain sin, but if our intent is truly to change our ways and overcome that sin, then God will give us the grace to do it. We cannot receive forgiveness from God without changing our ways.

God knows the difference between those who are sincere in their repentance and those who say they are sorry, just to temporarily ease their conscience. If someone comes to Him in sorrow, humility and sincerity, His grace is abundant.

Search your heart and ask God to give you the grace for true repentance and the power of the Holy Spirit to help you make the changes you need to make. True repentance is accompanied by corresponding action.

When we choose not to forgive someone, we are allowing that person to have power over us. The power that person has over us steals our thoughts and mind, and it makes us inactive and unproductive. The time spent thinking about the situation between us is unproductive and unfruitful; it delays and detours our destiny. We may want to hang onto the situation, but what we need to do is hand the person or incident over to God. Visualizing handing the person over to Jesus can be helpful in the deliverance process.

In the healing process, we must connect our emotions to our heart. An absence of heartfelt forgiveness can be a stumbling block to our deliverance. We need to allow our emotions to come forth, so speak forgiveness out loud: *Father God, I forgive* _____ *(insert person's name)*. Speak it out several times, until your emotions arise and you mean it or feel peace.

We desire revenge, but we need to be reminded that God is our avenger: "'Vengeance is Mine, I will repay,' says the Lord" (Romans 12:19). Our responsibility is to release love and to forgive. Unforgiveness can lead to medical issues like high blood pressure, stress and heart problems. I used to say, "I am choosing to forgive because I am leaving no room for the enemy to steal, kill and destroy and take me away from my husband, children and all the people I need to minister to."

Walking Out Your Deliverance

Healing can be a process. Let's walk through the process, do what is right in our heart and forgive others, so our Father will forgive us and we can start living the life of victory He intended. I have outlined some steps toward forgiveness you can take and some practical exercises you can do to assist you:

1. Write a list of names of the people who have hurt, betrayed, abandoned or offended you. Next, go outside and burn the list as a physical act of what you are releasing in the spiritual atmosphere. Handwritten lists are best, as writing them out gives you time to meditate and think. If you type the list on your computer, make

sure to delete the list after printing it, so you don't revisit the situation.

2. Write a letter expressing your feelings and disappointments. Pour out your emotions on paper to the person you need to forgive. Pray and ask the Holy Spirit for guidance. Afterward, burn the letter. Do not save a copy or mail the letter you wrote.

3. Meditate on forgiveness and what it means. Research Scriptures on forgiveness. Study instances where Jesus forgave others and offered you the ultimate forgiveness. Self-examine and reflect. Ask the Holy Spirit to search your heart and show you any unconfessed sin or any part you played in the dissension of a relationship.

Now that you have removed the blockages in your mind toward forgiving others, let's begin the process of forgiving ourselves, which is usually the hardest part. Take the following steps to accomplish that, speaking each thing out loud as you go down the list:

- I repent for _____. (Specifically name whatever you need to repent for.)
- Father, I ask Your forgiveness for _____. (Ask His forgiveness for each thing.)
- I forgive myself for_____. (If you cannot forgive yourself or you get stuck, or if this is hard to say, keep trying. Keep speaking it until you feel a release and feel that you have forgiven yourself.)
- I put my sin and unforgiveness at the foot of the cross and give it to You, Jesus. (Visualize putting them at His feet; He took them to the cross for you. Now see them on the cross and release them to Him.)
- I release my unforgiveness; I give it to You, Lord. I break agreement with unforgiveness in this situation. (There is

power in your words. When you break agreement with unforgiveness out loud, you will no longer hang onto it.)

Scriptures on Repentance and Forgiveness

Psalm 103:12; Isaiah 1:18; 43:25–26; Matthew 6:14–15; Luke
17:3–4; Acts 3:19; Ephesians 4:31–32; Colossians 3:13; 1 John 1:9

Prayer of Repentance and Forgiveness

There is power when we speak out into the spiritual atmosphere.
I encourage you to pray the prayers you find in these application
sections out loud throughout your healing process and in your
prayer time. Pray this prayer audibly to repent:

*Thank You for loving me, Father. Please forgive me for my
hardness of heart. Cleanse me of anything that is not of You.
Remove anger, hatred, bitterness, offense, rejection, resentment and anything else I have held onto. Help me receive
Your love, and in return, walk in Your love. Help me extend
the same forgiveness to myself and others that You have
given me, in Jesus' name. Amen!*

Now let's extend God's love and forgiveness to people in our lives
through audibly praying the following prayer:

*Heavenly Father, thank You for sending Your Son and my
Lord and Savior, Jesus Christ, to die for me. Thank You for
His example on the cross and His words, "Father, forgive
them, for they know not what they do." Father, this day I
choose to forgive those who have hurt, offended, abused
and betrayed me. I release forgiveness and offense. I ask You
to come in and saturate me with Your presence, allowing
me to feel love where there has been a void, emptiness and
numbness. Come in and soothe my heart, and heal my hurt*

and pain. Help me see others who have hurt me as You see them—as Your children, forgiven and loved. I choose this day to accept the atoning work of the cross and forgive these people in the mighty name of Your Son, Jesus Christ. Amen.

Spirits to Discern and Cast Out

Ask the Holy Spirit to reveal all the demonic spirits associated with unforgiveness that you need to cast out. Out loud, command these spirits to leave: "Spirit of _____, go, in Jesus' name!" You may have to do this several times over a period of time. Do it until you feel peace, a release or a spiritual shift. Spirits often associated with unforgiveness:

Accusation, anger, bitterness, condemnation, criticism, deception, deep hurt, defensiveness, discord, disrespect, distrust, hard-heartedness, hate, humiliation, jealousy, judgment, lying, manipulation, offense, resentment, retaliation, selfishness, soul ties, stubbornness, unfairness, unforgiveness, woundedness

Prayer of Activation

When we cast a spirit out, we need to make sure we fill the place it leaves in our soul with the Holy Spirit. One of the ways we can do that is by praying a prayer like the one that follows, asking the Holy Spirit to fill us. The second way we need to fill that place is by living a life filled with the continual presence of God through prayer, worship and Bible study. When you pray these activation prayers out loud, there is power in the words you speak.

Heavenly Father, I ask You to fill me up with the fruit of the Spirit. Fill me with love, joy, peace, longsuffering, kindness, goodness, faithfulness, gentleness and self-control (Galatians 5:22–23). Help me love others as You have loved me. Heal me, protect me and comfort me. I trust in You to be my Guide, my Companion and my Friend. Fill me to overflowing with Your

love for others, and help me have peace in abundance. I trust in
You for healing and restoration, in the name of Jesus. Amen.

There will be times when the enemy tries to attack your thought patterns, or when your mind will be distracted with negativity during the weeks following deliverance. You have God's truth and God's Word at your disposal, and they make up an arsenal with which you can conquer those thoughts. It is normal to experience some spiritual warfare attacks through the deliverance process and after receiving deliverance. Keep focused! The enemy will attempt to resist your deliverance. But remember, "He who is in you is greater than he who is in the world" (1 John 4:4).

Declarations to Speak Out

Speak out the following faith declarations and spiritual warfare declarations. Bookmark these pages and come back to them as often as necessary to assist you in renewing your mind, transforming your heart and increasing your faith.

Faith Declarations

Make these faith declarations audibly, with power and authority, believing that you will receive them. Speak them out from a position of *I have these*, not *I'm trying to obtain these*.

- God, I thank You that You are for me and that You put people in my life who will love me unconditionally. Help me receive their love.
- Lord, I listen to You. My ears and mind are attentive to You. When I focus my thoughts on You, feelings such as paranoia have no room to take hold. I know that You, God, are my defender. Every tongue that rises up against me in judgment will be condemned (Isaiah 54:17). I declare that I am victorious over vain imaginations.

41

- The *shalom* peace of God resides in me. I breathe in the presence of the Holy Spirit, and He refocuses my body, mind and soul. I command tension and stress to go now, in Jesus' name. I declare that the peace of God, which passes all understanding, surrounds me (Philippians 4:7).

- I take every thought captive and submit it to Christ. Negative, ungodly feelings do not line up with Christ's intentions for me. I therefore choose to dismiss them. I will not entertain negative thoughts. I bring every thought captive and submit it to the obedience of Christ (2 Corinthians 10:4–5).

- I will follow biblical instructions and choose to forgive again (Matthew 18:22). I know that Christ in me gives me the strength to forgive. I declare that I choose to love, and love is forgiving.

- The Son has set me free. I am therefore free indeed (John 8:36).

Spiritual Warfare Declarations

Make these spiritual warfare declarations audibly, with power and authority. When you speak out these declarations, you are taking up your God-given authority to bind and restrict the enemy and counteract future attacks. Declare them repeatedly, until you feel something release in the spiritual atmosphere.

- I command every spirit of offense and unforgiveness to leave me now. You have been released of your demonic assignment to infiltrate my soul, in Jesus' name.

- Spirits of dissension, disunity and disruption, I abort your mission against my relationships and destiny. Be removed and cast out of my life, in Jesus' name.

- Every negative cycle and pattern sent by demonic forces to repeat ungodly circumstances in my life, I remove your power, and I say that I am covered by the blood of the Lamb, that I am chosen and destined, and that you will immediately stop wreaking havoc on my life.

- Every evil deploy dispatched against my emotions and attempting to infiltrate my soul in a downward spiral, I command you to cease your attacks now, in Jesus' name.

- I penetrate the powers of darkness with the fire of God and speak into the spiritual atmosphere that I have victory over all things, and that I am a conqueror!

- I decree and declare that my life will change from this moment on, and I will capture every thought and not take in the offense.

- I speak, decree and command every emotional defilement against my soul that I was holding onto is now gone, and I am set free by the blood of the Lamb.

- My year will change; this is my season and my time to move in my prophetic destiny. I am no longer captive, but am set free, and I thank You, Lord Jesus, for a clear mind, in Your name.

Part 2

GETTING UNSHACKLED FROM 10 STRONGHOLDS

CHAPTER 3

FEAR

Self-Assessment—Spirit of Fear

On a scale of 1 to 10, rate each statement below.

1. I worry and stress about things that never happen.
2. I feel fear when a person needs to talk to me, and I automatically process out the worst scenario.
3. I have a fear of financial lack, being alone, not finding a spouse, or failure.
4. I have a fear of flying, heights, death, darkness, water, bridges, spiders, snakes, or the loss of a loved one, a pet or my job.
5. I can feel fear manifest inside me, and my body reacts with a physical manifestation.
6. I feel my mind get trapped and paralyzed in anxiety or negativity where I can't pull it back into a positive or edifying direction.
7. False scenarios, vain imaginations and negative or piercing conversations plague my thoughts.

I lived in fear for over 45 years. It was not paranoia or debilitating fear, but it did torment and traumatize me at times. I remember several occasions when fear would attack my mind. I would be stuck in a negative way of thinking, with fear, worry and anxiety attacks happening for a day or two at a time. I would try to pray, worship and do everything I knew how to do as a Christian, but the fear would bind my mind and pull me into thinking the worst about different situations. I knew the enemy was sending resistance against my destiny.

Over the years, there were also smaller fears I struggled with, such as walking in the dark at night and being afraid of thunderstorms. I remember being afraid to drive on bridges suspended over water, and I remember the freedom I felt when I drove sixteen miles over the Louisiana causeway with a smile on my face and joy in my heart because I could do it without fear. Freedom feels great!

Fear is an emotional reaction from trauma in our mind, or fear is a spiritual stronghold that has built up over time. Fear binds our mind into thinking about what we fear. It grips us. It causes us to think in a direction our mind should not focus on. To remove fear from our lives, we must first recognize its components.

How Fear Makes Us Feel and Respond

Fear makes us feel and respond a number of different ways. Can you identify from this list how you respond to fear?

- Fear shuts down our emotions and makes us feel numb.
- Fear prevents us from walking in our God-given destiny.
- Fear impedes our worship, in fear of what others will think.
- Fear distracts us.

- Fear interrupts our sleep at night.
- Fear lies to us that our loved ones won't forgive us, so we keep hidden secrets.
- Fear stirs paranoia so that we avoid something we need to do, thinking we will be left with a negative outcome.
- Fear brings forth doubt, unbelief and negativity so that we are thinking the worst about situations and outcomes.

Fear encompasses us and binds us into thinking about what we fear, pulling our mind in the wrong direction. When we suffer from fear, our minds will think the worst and go in directions that are unlike us. Fear will pull us into thinking negatively about a subject, which causes us to worry. Fear causes us to question our faith and the solidity of the Word of God we want to stand on.

When fear attacks, it is binding because it co-labors with a mind-binding spirit. When fear comes upon us strongly, we feel a pull to think in a direction contrary to what we believe. Seducing spirits and thoughts (not seducing in the sexual sense, but seducing in the sense of luring us) draw us into thinking in the very way we are trying to rebuke. It is difficult to resist the pull, and we find ourselves unable to control where our thoughts are heading. Identifying how lying, mind-binding or seducing and luring spirits are behind the strongman of fear is key to our freedom.

Knowing fear's components allows us to rebuke it and take authority over our thoughts, bringing them back into alignment with the Word of God. We cannot, however, take authority over that which we don't know is plaguing us. Unless you cast out the mind-binding, lying and seducing spirits, fear will keep attacking you. Ultimately, the root cause of fear is negativity, which is behind thoughts such as:

- *You're going to get robbed if you go down that alley.*
- *You're going to get in an accident if you turn down that road.*

- *You aren't going to have enough money to pay rent.*
- *Your spouse (or child or friend) is lying to you.*

These can be some of the lies, thoughts or vain imaginations that you hear in your mind. What makes you rise in fear? What thoughts do you hear? What makes your heart beat faster, your adrenaline increase and fear enter your body? You can feel fear enter your body. You can feel it rise within you. Fear makes your insides tremble and vibrate; you can feel fear physically grip you.

How can you take your thoughts captive to conquer your fear? When lying spirits and thoughts come upon you, you need to capture these thoughts instantly in order to overcome them and be delivered. The apostle Paul said,

> For though we walk in the flesh, we do not war according to the flesh. For the weapons of our warfare are not carnal but mighty in God for pulling down strongholds, casting down arguments and every high thing that exalts itself against the knowledge of God, bringing every thought into captivity to the obedience of Christ.
>
> 2 Corinthians 10:3–5

It is possible to take our thoughts captive and dismiss them; the problem is, we don't do it. When our minds feel locked down with negativity, worry and stress, we start thinking things contrary to the Word of God. When this happens, it is time for us get up and get busy capturing our thoughts and filling ourselves with faith.

Don't sit and think and rot and stink. Get involved in an activity that will cause your mind to disengage from ungodly thoughts. Worship! Pray! Read your Bible! Do something you have to think about, so that your mind will be released from cycling through wrong thoughts. Don't sit and meditate on wrong thoughts; doing so entertains them and plagues your mind. If your mind is not busy, it will stay focused on wrong thoughts. Get up, take authority over the attack coming at you, and conquer those emotions and spiritual strongholds.

God's Love Conquers Fear

We need to know the depths of God's love so we don't carry fear. The Bible says, "There is no fear in love; but perfect love casts out fear, because fear involves torment. But he who fears has not been made perfect in love" (1 John 4:18). When we know and recognize God's love, we can trust Him. We need to trust that His love for us is perfect and that He will take care of us. When we don't trust God, we fear our natural circumstances. God is love; therefore, when we have God's love, no torment or fear should reside in us because we are full of His love.

We need to take on love and faith instead of fear. If we trust God, we will not give in to fear because we know God is our protector and defender. He is greater than any fear the enemy can attack us with: "For God has not given us a spirit of fear, but of power and of love and of a sound mind" (2 Timothy 1:7). The Word also says, "And the LORD, He is the One who goes before you. He will be with you, He will not leave you nor forsake you; do not fear nor be dismayed" (Deuteronomy. 31:8). If we believe that God will not leave us, then we should not be afraid.

What we need is a faith increase. Psalm 91 is a great place to find a faith increase in how God is our protector and defender. We are increasing our faith to believe that we can actually live without fear. We don't have to live with fear; however, many of us have been gripped by fear most of our lives and are trying desperately to be set free from it. No matter how big or small the fear is, we can and should be free from it.

How do you know if you just don't like steep places and severe drop-offs, versus having a fear of them? When we look at Niagara Falls and the Grand Canyon, we may experience a fear of heights. I remember that when I had a spirit of fear and went to the edge in such a place, I would feel fear grip me on the inside. It would pierce me, and I could feel it penetrate throughout my body. That kind of reaction is a spirit of fear. After I was delivered of fear, my husband and I went to Tahquamenon Falls in Upper Michigan and I no longer felt fear grip my insides. While I still may not like high places, I am no longer afraid.

Discovering Fear's Entry Points

Discovering and exploring the ways fear enters us and how to break it off from its original entry point (which is the root cause) will assist us in closing the doors to it. As we go back and find the stronghold in our life or the way that fear entered, we can repent, renounce the fear, break our agreement with it and eradicate it from our lives. Some ways fear initially enters us are through generational curses, soul ties, near-death experiences, trauma (whether emotional or physical) and accidents. Let's look at these a little more closely.

Generational curses

Generational curses come from our family line. Growing up, we take on our parents' character traits and habits. If our parents experience fear, they can say or do things that will impart fear to us. As children, we may not have been taught about the spiritual realm and so may not have known how to avoid taking on the ungodly habits and behavioral patterns of our parents. As children, we don't realize that some of the things they say or the way they are raising us is exposing us to strongholds.

As parents, we need to be careful to seek out inner healing and deliverance so we don't impart our negative habits and strongholds to our children. As we control our emotions and our reactions to situations, we will be teaching our children not to respond negatively. When we impart positivity and faith instead of fear, we assist our children in conquering negative situations they face in a positive way.

Getting rid of generational curses is not as simple as laying hands on someone and commanding that all generational curses be gone, in Jesus' name. We need to work out our generational curses through a time of inner healing, seeking God and changing our attitudes, behavioral patterns and habits. We need to cast out specific generational curses, saying, for example, "spirit of fear, be gone, in Jesus' name" or "spirit of anger, be gone, in Jesus' name."[1]

Soul ties

Soul ties are hindrances we experience because we have been in a relationship with another person. We can get a soul-tie attachment from a friend, a lover or someone with whom we have had sexual relations. It can happen through any relationship where we have been emotionally or physically involved.

Identify whether or not you have a soul-tie issue by asking yourself, *Am I reacting, saying something or feeling some way that is out of character for me?* Suppose you have never thrived on getting other people's attention, but you have a friend or multiple friends around you who love attention and act out pridefully. You can tell when they are acting out in pride and attention seeking, and you have thought to yourself, *I'm not like that.* Then suddenly you find yourself also acting out in pride and desiring attention. Those actions would indicate a soul-tie attachment, a demonic spirit harassing you. You can take authority over it like this: "Soul-tie spirit of attention or pride, go, in Jesus' name!"

Trauma

Fear creates emotional trauma from which we need to receive healing. Trauma is often something we overlook, not realizing the huge impact it has on us. Looking back to discover where the trauma entered will assist us in repentance if we were at fault, or forgiveness if another person was responsible for our trauma. Releasing repentance and forgiveness will lead to healing the trauma within our soul.

1. See my book *Discerning and Destroying the Works of Satan* (Destiny Image, 2018) for more on deliverance from generational curses.

To receive healing, we don't need to relive the trauma. We need to find the entry point and what caused us to be fearful, or pinpoint why an experience was so traumatic for us. If we can discover why we still react the same way to a similar situation even though it is years later, we can prevent the same response from happening again after we have gone through the healing process.

We do not simply want to claim that we are afraid of something and accept that it is part of life to live in fear of certain things. There is a difference between fear and not liking something. I have a friend who does not like spiders, so I decided to have a little fun with her. I brought her a bag one day and said, "I have a gift for you." Then I pulled some fake spiders out of the bag as a gag.

What I did not realize is that this friend could not even look at fake spiders! She covered her eyes, horrified, and exclaimed, "Put them away!"

Being a deliverance minister, I noticed that beyond just not liking spiders, she was actually afraid of them. I wanted to bring forth healing and decided to pry a little, so I asked a few questions and found out that when she was young, someone had played a practical joke on her with spiders. Since then, she has been severely tormented by the fear of them. A spirit of trauma and fear had entered her through that childhood prank, and now she needed deliverance.

Near-death experiences

Near-death experiences such as attempting suicide, drowning, getting into a life-threatening vehicle accident or facing medical emergencies are entry points for fear and trauma. Fear is usually the first reaction we find ourselves experiencing when we later engage in activities similar to whatever caused us to suffer the trauma. Being close to death can cripple us and paralyze our emotions. It is an area of fear and trauma in which we need to seek healing.

Accidents

In fear of something happening again, we often don't want to reengage in an experience in which a traumatic incident occurred. We cannot live in fear of a reoccurrence, however. If we do, it will prevent us from having fun or taking part in normal activities in which we need to participate. I once knew of a parent who fell into a fire pit accidentally, and from then on would not allow any family members, especially the children, anywhere near a campfire. This is an example of allowing fear to paralyze you and prevent you from doing something, in fear that it will happen again. We need to conquer our fears by confronting them and putting ourselves in a similar situation again.

There is a saying, "If you fall off the horse, get back in the saddle." My daughter, Lauren, literally has fallen off her horse, and that is exactly what she does. She immediately gets back in the saddle, and she does it as a precautionary measure, so she does not give fear a foothold.

The Bible instructs us not to fear: "For you did not receive the spirit of bondage again to fear, but you received the Spirit of adoption by whom we cry out, 'Abba, Father'" (Romans 8:15). We are adopted daughters and sons of the Most High God. We have been given a new bloodline—the bloodline of Jesus Christ! He does not fear. We need to know who we are in Christ so that we can conquer fear.

Jesus has empowered us and equipped us; therefore, we should not fear. When fear tries to creep in and I start thinking about the generational curse of fear that was part of me, I say to myself, *I am an adopted daughter of the Most High God.* I remind myself that I am not a product of my past. I am no longer captive to fear. I tell myself, *I am adopted. Generational curses are a thing of the past. My heavenly Father has adopted me into His bloodline, and now I have a royal line without curses and fear.*

Quoting Romans 8:15 has renewed my mind and has brought me great freedom. I am an heir to the throne, and so are you. There is no fear in the bloodline of an heir to the throne. An heir to the throne has been born and raised to inherit the throne. By renewing our minds about our Kingdom inheritance, we will no longer be slaves to our past, the way we were raised or the thoughts that plague us. Changing our mentality and renewing our mind are both keys to knowing we are heirs to a throne, without curses, demonic attacks or unhealthy thoughts. We have the bloodline of Jesus Christ, and He does not fear.

Throughout the Bible, we see the words *fear not* or *do not fear*. One of the best ways we can obtain freedom in the area of fear is to quote Scripture and renew our mind against fear. Declare these Scriptures out loud in faith to yourself right now:

> Be strong and of good courage, do not fear nor be afraid of them; for the LORD your God, He is the One who goes with you. He will not leave you nor forsake you.
>
> Deuteronomy 31:6

> Therefore we will not fear, even though the earth be removed, and though the mountains be carried into the midst of the sea.
>
> Psalm 46:2

Trusting God

Trusting God to take care of us and those we love is important in eradicating fear from our lives. I believe we all have a level of fear that needs to be dismantled in our thinking. Jesus came to set the captives free. Fear can arise in a moment, and false scenarios and vain imaginations can plague our minds. When we fear, anxiety can also be our first reaction. Negativity and anxiety cause worry and stress, which results in fear becoming a stronghold.

Instead of reacting in the negative, we need to react in the positive. Instead of reacting with fear, we need to react in faith. When our credit card statement comes in the mail, we need to trust that

God will provide all our needs, as long as we are living biblically and not being foolish. We need to claim that our children are covered with the blood of Christ, and that "No weapon formed against you shall prosper" (Isaiah 54:17). We need to respond with faith, claim the Word of God over our lives, and not fear. Instead of rising in fear, we need to rise up and be faith giants!

Fearful reactions are not natural and are different than being concerned. Can you identify the difference between concern and fearful reactions in your life? Our first reaction should not be to think the worst. That is fear, not faith. When we know who God is, we know He will take care of us. We should be praying on the offense for our employment, income and family, not on the defense. It doesn't mean that bad things are not going to happen, but we will have peace amidst the storm when we trust in God.

Part of growing in faith and being released from fear is knowing who we are in Christ. We realize who we are by studying, believing and living out the Word of God. The Word says, "Though an army may encamp against me, my heart shall not fear; though war may rise against me, in this I will be confident" (Psalm 27:3). Look at this Scripture's instruction: "in this I will be confident." Yes, something may rise against us. But we will not fear, and we will be confident in the God who created us, the God who made us, the God who loves us. We need to put our trust and confidence in Him, not in ourselves or another person. We need to be confident in the fact that God is who He says He is and does what His Word says He does.

When we experience fear about financial provision, we need to look at Scriptures like Matthew 10:31: "Do not fear therefore; you are of more value than many sparrows." If God takes care of the sparrows and provides food for them, will He not provide for us? He loves to clothe us, feed us and house us. He cares for us more than for the sparrows. When you look back, you can see how the Lord provided for you.

Why do we worry about something we can't control? When we are in a difficult financial situation, we need to trust in Jehovah

Jireh, the God who is our provider. Worrying and allowing fear to creep in and overtake the situation never changes anything. When we take in fear, we start operating in the flesh and not in the Spirit. We need to walk in the Spirit and tune in to what the Spirit of the Lord is saying, so we can effectively walk out our faith. When we are in prayer and heed His voice, He will instruct us about how to change our financial situation. Declare these Scriptures out loud in faith. Do it two or three times!

> In God (I will praise His word), in God I have put my trust; I will not fear. What can flesh do to me?
>
> Psalm 56:4

> The LORD is on my side; I will not fear. What can man do to me?
>
> Psalm 118:6

Fear of Man

A lot of fear comes from thinking about other people's reactions. We can fear not being accepted. We can fear that people are going to hurt us, or not like our ideas or what we believe in. Our fear can come from what others might think. We fear how we should worship if people are watching, whether or not we should raise our hands or what someone will think if we lay prostrate on the floor or at the altar.

We spend too much time wondering what other people will think, and it ends up putting fear in us about how to act. Even though some of these fears may seem minor, we don't have to allow ourselves to live in bondage to them. We can be delivered from all spirits and bondages of fear! A lot of our fear is self-inflicted from our perception of what people think, or from rejection we have suffered in relationships. Fear is a battlefield of the mind. When we fear someone's reaction, often it is our thoughts and perceptions about how the person will perceive what we said or did. Our imagination and fleshly thoughts prevent us from acting out, because we fear what others will think.

When we give in to such fears, we don't see the reality of a situation. The only one we need to fear is God, with a healthy, reverential fear of our Lord and heavenly Father. God is our vindicator. The Bible says, "You must not fear them, for the LORD your God Himself fights for you" (Deuteronomy 3:22). When another person or the enemy comes against us, we need to know that God will fight for us. We are His children, and when we are in right standing with Him, He has our back. The Bible also says, "Then your light shall break forth like the morning, your healing shall spring forth speedily, and your righteousness shall go before you; the glory of the LORD shall be your rear guard" (Isaiah 58:8). God is our rear guard, side guard and front guard. He is going to take care of us, protect us and keep us. We need to trust Him and believe what His Word says.

Releasing the Fear of Man

God is our helper. Hebrews 13:6 says, "So we may boldly say: "The LORD is my helper; I will not fear. What can man do to me?" We need to realize that He goes before us. He knows what will happen. He knows the persecution we will face. He knows when people will come up against us and when we will meet resistance.

Often, after we go through a trial or struggle, we see God's hand in it. I am not saying that God caused it, but that He helped us pass through it and grow spiritually in the process.

We don't need to fear difficult times—not when we know God is our helper and we can trust Him. We can trust Him and not fear, because the Holy Spirit resides within us. First Corinthians 3:16 reminds us, "Do you not know that you are the temple of God and that the Spirit of God dwells in you?"

The Holy Spirit lives within us! If the Spirit of God lives in us (and He does), He does not fear. If no fear lives in the Spirit of the Lord, then no fear should live in us.

Possess Your Land

In Deuteronomy, the Israelites are told to go in and possess their physical Promised Land: "Look, the LORD your God has set the land before you; go up and possess it, as the LORD God of your fathers has spoken to you; do not fear or be discouraged" (Deuteronomy 1:21). We need to possess the land of our mind. We need to get violent and diligent in taking our thoughts captive. The words *possess the land* are action words. They mean we have something to do. We have to get aggressive in our fight with the enemy and our own vain imaginations, and take back the territory in our mind that has been infiltrated with wrong thinking.

If you want something, go fight for it. Be diligent about making it come to pass. I don't know anything more important than possessing the land of our mind so we can have the freedom Christ intended us to have. How do we possess our mind? How do we apply this principle to daily living? We meditate on the good things, as Scripture instructs:

> Finally, brethren, whatever things are true, whatever things are noble, whatever things are just, whatever things are pure, whatever things are lovely, whatever things are of good report, if there is any virtue and if there is anything praiseworthy—meditate on these things.
>
> Philippians 4:8

Refocus your mind. When it goes in the wrong direction, meditate on Scriptures, or think about a positive experience or something that relaxes you. Keep pressing in, and try to think positively in order to push your mind and thoughts in a pleasing direction.

We need to take our thoughts captive and say, "No, I'm not going to think that way." We need to speak out loud and rebuke the enemy, because there is power in our words. Faith comes by hearing, and we need to speak out faith to capture our thoughts. When the enemy attempts to come against your mind, take authority by speaking out, "I rebuke that thought, in Jesus' name. I call forth a mind transformation. I speak and declare that only positive thoughts enter my mind. I call forth peace to permeate my mind."

Recognizing how the enemy speaks to you and torments you with fear will assist you in taking these thoughts captive. Cancel any assignments sent by the enemy, and speak Scripture over yourself. Speak life, truth and the peace of God into your mind. This is how you take possession of your mind and make it God's territory.

The enemy used to torment me with fear of accidents and fear that something was wrong with my vehicle. I would get in my vehicle, hear strange noises and see warning lights going off for no reason. When these things happened, fear would creep in because I always wanted a good, working vehicle to get my children and myself safely where we needed to go. I was learning to use my authority in Christ when I started speaking to my vehicle, telling it to work properly. I would command the warning lights to go off, and I would plead the blood of Jesus over my drive time.

I know some of you may be thinking that vehicles wear out and check-engine lights go on for our safety and protection when something is wrong. I do believe that's true. But when you go on a two-thousand-mile trip to do street evangelism and your temperature gauge keeps going in the red but your vehicle does not overheat, and when every service station you stop at tells you nothing is wrong, then the issue is the enemy wreaking havoc on the plans of God to spread the Gospel. I was four hours from home, sitting in the last dealership I stopped at, when the mechanic showed me the test readings and tried to convince me, "Ma'am, there's nothing wrong with your vehicle!"

That's when I replied, "Do you believe in demons?" The mechanic was not quite sure how to reply to that.

It took a while before I walked in complete freedom from fearing problems with my vehicle. I still don't like things going wrong with it, but they no longer cause fear, and that is the difference. Our vehicles will break down, tires will go flat and brakes will need replacing. The difference is that when these things happen, they no longer cause fear to rise up and grip me.

Walking Out Your Deliverance

When we practice how Christ would think and react, it will prevent fear from plaguing our souls. We need to renew our minds to have the mind of Christ and remember that we are made in His image, without fear. Try journaling about where you can and cannot trust God, and then allow the Holy Spirit to help you evaluate and work out your deliverance from the revelation you receive.

Scriptures on Faith

Psalm 23:4; 34:4; Proverbs 3:5–6; Matthew 6:34; John 14:1, 27; Romans 15:13; 2 Timothy 1:7; Hebrews 11:1

Prayer of Repentance and Forgiveness

Pray this prayer audibly to repent and release forgiveness:

Heavenly Father, I ask You to forgive me for any thoughts I have received in the spiritual or natural that have contributed to a spirit of fear. I choose to forgive anyone who has brought fear upon me. Fear is not from You, heavenly Father.

I therefore release fear from my life. I break agreement with the spirit of fear that has kept me in bondage. In the mighty name of Jesus, I restrict the strongman of fear from activating against my life. I command any ungodly soul ties or generational curses of fear to go now, in the name of Jesus. I command all tormenting, mind-binding and lying spirits to go, in Jesus' name. I command spirits of trauma

to leave me, and all strongman spirits of fear to go now,
in Jesus' name.
Father, I thank You that You make me new and that I no
longer have to live in bondage to fear.
Jesus, I thank You for dying on the cross and taking away
my fear so that I can live in freedom and faith. In Your name,
I pray. Amen.

Spirits to Discern and Cast Out

Ask the Holy Spirit to reveal all the demonic spirits associated
with fear that you need to cast out. Out loud, command these spirits
to leave: "Spirit of _____, go, in Jesus' name!" You may have
to do this several times over a period of time. Do it until you feel
peace, a release or a spiritual shift. Spirits often associated with fear:

Accident, anxiety, bondage, death, distrust, double-mindedness,
doubt, fear, generational curses, lying, mind-binding, nightmares,
paranoia, passivity, phobias, soul ties, stress, torment, trauma,
trembling, turmoil, vain imaginations, worry

Prayer of Activation

In the name of Jesus, I receive the shalom peace of God.
Lord, I ask You to help me trust You. I seek You for a supernatural impartation of faith. I invite You, Holy Spirit, to fill
me to overflowing. I declare that I am overflowing with the
peace of God that surpasses all understanding. I thank You,
Holy Spirit, that You never leave me, but that You co-labor
with me to bring me peace and trust.
I thank You, Jesus, for dying on the cross and taking my
fear so that I can live with Your peace.
I declare that I have a sound mind full of powerful, positive thoughts from the Word of God. I commit to capture
every thought and no longer to give fear a foothold in my
life, in the name of Jesus, I pray. Amen.

Declarations to Speak Out

Speak out the following faith declarations and spiritual warfare declarations. Bookmark these pages and come back to them as often as necessary to assist you in renewing your mind, transforming your heart and increasing your faith.

Faith Declarations

Make these faith declarations audibly, with power and authority, believing that you will receive them. Speak them out from a position of *I have these*, not *I'm trying to obtain these*. While you transition from fear to faith, read these declarations out regularly to help you grow strong in faith and renew your mind.

- I declare and decree that my mind is being renewed and transformed day by day!
- I proclaim that as the enemy tries to attack and infiltrate my thoughts, I will use those trials as a building block for my faith. I will learn from every test and trial and use what I have endured to make me stronger in my faith.
- I take authority over my mind and thoughts. When negative thoughts come in, I submit them to the Word of God and take those thoughts captive, dismissing them immediately.
- I refuse to take in the enemy's lies of fear, torment and trauma. I proclaim and believe that Jesus has given me a spirit of love, power, faith and peace.
- I proclaim that I will focus on what is godly and good. I will not focus on the negative. When my mind wants to head in an ungodly direction, I will get up and occupy my mind with prayer, worship and the Word.
- I believe my mind is being renewed daily. The Holy Spirit resides in me; therefore, I will seek Him for direction and

instruction on how I can change my thoughts and grow in my faith.

- I decree that I will not act or react in the natural or in my flesh. I will choose to walk in the Spirit and co-labor with Him in all I do, say and think.
- I declare that I will not be unproductive or unfruitful in my thinking. I have the mind of Christ because the Spirit of God dwells in me.
- I declare and decree that I am made in the image of my Father, and since there is no fear in God, there is no fear in me.
- I speak peace over my life and declare this day that I have received and am walking in the freedom and fullness of Christ, in Jesus' name.

Spiritual Warfare Declarations

Make these spiritual warfare declarations audibly, with power and authority. When you speak out these declarations, you are taking up your God-given authority to bind and restrict the enemy and counteract future attacks. Declare them repeatedly, until you feel something release in the spiritual atmosphere.

- I bind, rebuke and annihilate every spirit of fear attempting to come against me and my family line. I say you are cut off from your life source and you will not invade my family or my thoughts!
- I call off every assignment of the enemy to invade my thoughts with negativity, fear and paranoia. I decree and declare that I have a sound mind, and I think right, good and edifying thoughts.
- I rebuke every attack of the enemy against me to put fear into me. I speak and decree that I have not been given a spirit of fear, but of love, power and a sound mind. I have discipline and self-control to conquer my thoughts!

- I command every spiritual warfare attack against my life that is creating fear, stress, worry and anxiety to cease to exist. I call off every assignment from the enemy sent to create confusion in my thinking.
- I speak and decree that I am secure in God. He is my safety and refuge. He is my protector, and I will trust in Him.
- Every demonic entity sent to create destruction in my life and distract me from my destiny, I command your assignment to cease to exist, in Jesus' name! I have been given an abundant life filled with Jesus' light and love. I will complete the commission He has for me!
- I command no retribution from the enemy over my life for the freedom I am pursuing. I will walk forward in strength, trust and peace, in Jesus' name. Amen!
- I thank You and praise You, Lord, for the mind freedom and renewal I have received, and I command complete freedom to come forth, in Your name.

CHAPTER 4

INTIMIDATION

Self-Assessment—Spirit of Intimidation

On a scale of 1 to 10, rate each statement below.

1. I keep quiet instead of speaking out, in fear of what people will think.

2. I worry about people's reactions if I do certain things.

3. I hold back in worship, dancing, raising my hands or singing at the top of my lungs because I am concerned with how another person will respond.

4. I hold back in gifts of the Spirit like releasing a prophetic word or praying healing for a person, in fear of being wrong.

5. I withdraw when I perceive how a person will react to my actions.

6. I stuff my feelings and keep quiet instead of speaking out, because I am afraid people won't value what I say or it will cause an argument.

7. I keep myself in a safe place instead of taking risks, in fear of what others will think.

Intimidation can be defined as the act of rendering people timid or inspiring them with fear. Intimidation affects most of us. One kind of intimidation comes when a person you know purposely tries to intimidate you. This could be someone in authority, a spouse, a church leader, a family member or a boss. This person usually has a controlling and dominating spirit. He or she could be consciously or subconsciously putting fear upon you. When exuding intimidation, such people will purposefully say things that reinforce their superiority.

Intimidation is the action of intimidating or making afraid. When someone intimidates us, we are afraid to do something we want to do. We are usually aware that we are being held back from taking action in some way, but we do not acknowledge it as intimidation. Intimidation overwhelms us with fear and inferiority, and it leads to confusion, lack of faith and fear of confrontation. Whether we know someone is intimidating us or not, when we are intimidated it restrains us from action and forces us into submission to that person.

Intimidation Blocks the Gifts

Intimidation prevents us from operating in the gifts of the Spirit God has given us. The way we pray for a person for healing might not be the way someone else prays, so when others are around, we often hesitate and stand back from praying for people because we fear what others will think. Even though no one is trying to intimidate us on purpose in that situation, when we refrain from taking action in fear of what someone will think, it is still intimidation.

God has given us good gifts to use for the edification of the Kingdom and the advancement of ministry. When we live in fear of using them, we lose our proficiency at operating in them. Because of inadequacy and insecurity, we can find ourselves not releasing the gifts as often as the Spirit leads us to. But the gifts can be stirred up again, as Paul tells Timothy: "Therefore I remind you to stir up the gift of God which is in you through the laying on of my hands" (2 Timothy 1:6). We should want to keep the gifts active.

When I first started to prophesy, I had to practice. I had to use that gifting continually in order to increase in it and test my accuracy at delivering a word and hearing from the Spirit of the Lord. As I released the gift more, I grew in my ability and confidence to release it.

I remember being intimidated when I would prophesy in front of my overseer. An overseer is someone who agrees to help us grow and develop spiritually; he or she offers wise counsel and holds us accountable for our ministry operation and personal growth. When my overseer was present in certain ministry situations, I would become timid and not as bold as I usually was. I was secure and confident when I prophesied without him around. With him around, I was intimidated into releasing prophecy because I knew he was observing me and listening.

Intimidation can manifest that way when we minister alongside our pastor or an overseer. These men and women are sent to minister beside us and pull out and develop our giftings, not make us anxious. Yet we may feel we have to perform a certain way or put more power and authority into our ministry time when we are with them. We start operating in our flesh, trying to impress them because we are intimidated, or we get nervous and cower back in fear. This should not be our normal reaction. We need to be ourselves and allow the Spirit to flow through us. As He does, we should receive gladly any correction or insight our overseer has to add, knowing those insights will develop us to minister at a deeper level.

Insecurity in Our Prayer Time

Prayer is another area where we hold ourselves back when we are ministering alongside a prayer warrior or intercessor who is spiritually stronger than we are. We hear someone belt out what we consider a powerful, eloquent prayer, and we feel we have to compete with it, or we feel inadequate about what we were just about to release. It happens in that moment when it's your turn to pray and the thought going through your mind is, *I hope I can pray a prayer that sounds as good, or better.*

God has given us all different gifts. I remember one time when our team went to dinner with our overseer and his team. We had this great waiter who was a Christian. He said, "I'll pray for your food for you."

We said, "Okay."

He said, "Are you ready?"

We said, "Yes."

He said, "Say thank You."

We said, "Thank You."

He said, "Amen."

It really was rather cute and funny, but totally sincere. He taught us a lesson because he had been taught to pray with simplicity. When we concern ourselves with whether or not our prayer is good enough to pray in front of another person, it is intimidation.

The Bible says, "For God has not given us a spirit of fear, but of power and of love and of a sound mind" (2 Timothy 1:7). When you break this verse down and look at the context, it says in effect that God has not given us a spirit of intimidation. Studying the Bible and knowing the deeper definitions of the words it uses will assist us in bringing forth deeper revelation that we can apply.

I think the verse I just quoted gets overused, however, in the sense that we get so busy decreeing constantly what we don't have (a spirit of fear or intimidation) that we don't see what we do have to offer. When we focus too much on evil spirits and the negative, we don't focus enough on the positive and what God *has* given us. Our focus should be that we have a spirit of power and of love. When we have power and love, intimidation and fear should not arise. Part of having a sound mind is focusing on the right things. Instead of focusing on the fact that you have not been given a spirit of fear or intimidation, try focusing on what you have been given—power and love.

Intimidation Causes Compromise

Intimidation paralyzes us and causes us to compromise what we know is right. When we listen to gossip or negativity, we then don't stand up to it or stop it. We should shut it down, but we are intimidated about speaking out. Yet you and I are responsible for what we allow into our ear gates and eye gates. If someone is talking negatively about another person around you and you are not part of the problem or the solution, shut it down. Say kindly, "This conversation is not edifying," or "I'm not part of the problem or the solution, so I shouldn't participate in this conversation."

Take a bold stand! You may fear what another person will think if you shut down a conversation. But whom are you serving, God or man? When we don't stand up for our beliefs, we are serving man instead of God. We have to get past ourselves and what people think of us, and be bold enough to shut conversations down and not compromise our beliefs.

When we are intimidated, it paralyzes us from speaking out what we want, ministering the way we want and acting how we want. Even though we are not always consciously aware that we are being intimidated, we are. When we are intimidated, we truly are being controlled in the spiritual realm because it is holding us back from taking action. We need boldness, not intimidation. Boldness is a popular prayer request. You can't truly operate in boldness, however, until you discover the root that hinders your boldness. Ask yourself, *Why am I afraid to speak out? Why am I afraid to shut down a negative conversation?*

You serve whomever you obey and fear. "For do I now persuade men, or God? Or do I seek to please men? For if I still pleased men, I would not be a bondservant of Christ" (Galatians 1:10). When someone is intimidating us, we yield our power and authority to that person. We are in essence saying, "What you think and want is more important than what I think or want, or more important than what God thinks or wants." When we refrain from taking action because of an intimidating person, we subconsciously give that person control over us. Fear of man will hold us back and prevent us from operating in the fullness of God.

Many people are overly concerned with what other people will think about their situations. That is true when we are asking ourselves, *What will* _____ *think?* Our first concern should not be what others think of our actions, but what God thinks. We need some healthy, reverential fear of the Lord. Are we here to please men or please God?

Intimidation Seeks Control

People with impure motives and hidden agendas will seek to intimidate others on purpose in order to maintain control. Once when I was ministering somewhere, a powerful move of God came into that place. The ministry leaders were intimidated that we were moving in such a powerful anointing, so to reverse the situation, they attempted to intimidate us. The first night, I experienced such a disruption in the spiritual realm that I stayed up and prayed until 5:00 a.m. Through that, I heard the Lord specifically instruct me to pray to close the mouth of the devourer.

The next night as we appeared early for another event, the ministry leaders confronted us and said they wanted to meet first. We went into a private area with them, and then we stared at each other for 45 minutes. They could not open their mouths to say anything! They were the ones who had pulled us aside to speak to us—wanting to intimidate us. But their mouths were bound by what the Holy Spirit had instructed me to pray and speak out. They were using intimidation to control us, but praise the Lord, it did not work.

Intimidation can cause us to yield our authority to a controlling person. When we are intimidated and yield our authority instead of operating in it, we are afraid to do the thing we are supposed to be doing. God gave Adam authority. Everything was perfect before Adam and Eve sinned; there was no disease, no poverty and no war. When Adam sinned, he compromised what was perfect. He yielded his place and position in the spiritual realm. He yielded his authority, which affected everything underneath his authority. God did not come into the Garden and restore it, because it had been given to Adam. It was no longer God's to restore.

Years later, however, God sent His Son, Jesus, to restore mankind's place of dominion (authority). Upon His resurrection, Jesus transferred His authority back to us. I like to call it His power of attorney. When we are someone's power of attorney, we have the right to sign for and operate on behalf of that person. When Jesus was here on earth, He said, "All authority has been given to Me in heaven and on earth" (Matthew 28:18). God sent His Son to right what Adam had done wrong, so that the authority He had originally given mankind would be ours again.

Don't Succumb to Intimidation

When I read the prophet Elijah's story in the book of 1 Kings, I think, *This man had power, boldness and authority!* In the beginning, Elijah had no fear, no intimidation. It took courage and faith to go in front of a godless king like Ahab, an evil king who worshiped Baal. But Elijah went in front of him and commanded, "As the LORD God of Israel lives, before whom I stand, there shall not be dew nor rain these years, except at my word" (1 Kings 17:1).

During this time of drought, God provided for Elijah in a miraculous way, sending ravens to feed him near a brook that flowed into the Jordan. Then when the brook dried up, God led Elijah to a widow who would provide for him (see 1 Kings 17:2–16). Elijah then went out and killed hundreds of false prophets. Afterward, God gave him the supernatural strength to outrun Ahab's chariot (see 1 Kings 18:20–46).

This is a great story of victory. Elijah was provided with food and water supernaturally, he killed many false prophets, and then he had the strength to outrun King Ahab's chariot. But on the same day that Elijah won the battle with the prophets, he ran for his life because he allowed Queen Jezebel's words and reputation to intimidate him:

> Then Jezebel sent a messenger to Elijah, saying, "So let the gods do to me, and more also, if I do not make your life as the life of one of them [the false prophets] by tomorrow about this time." And when he saw that, he arose and ran for his life, and went to Beersheba, which belongs to Judah, and left his servant there.
>
> But he himself went a day's journey into the wilderness, and came and sat down under a broom tree. And he prayed that he might die, and said, "It is enough! Now, Lord, take my life, for I am no better than my fathers!"
>
> 1 Kings 19:2–4

In verse 4, Elijah wanted the Lord to take his life. God had provided for him over and over, but Elijah allowed Jezebel's words to intimidate him, and fear arose within him. We can experience the same thing. A person's words can intimidate us even when there is no real threat. We need to take every thought captive (see 2 Corinthians 10:4–5) and not give the enemy an inch of our mind and so allow intimidating thoughts to appear real. The battlefield is in our mind. If you can get control of your mind, you can win the battle.

Elijah experienced intimidation and withdrew. Even though he had experienced victory, in a sense it was lost because he allowed intimidation to shake him. Then God instructed Elijah to go and anoint Jehu as king over Israel, and to anoint Elisha as a prophet in his place (see 1 Kings 19:16–18). God had to send someone else to do what Elijah had been called to do. When we don't do what we know we are supposed to do because of intimidation, we surrender our authority to the person intimidating us.

Jehu and Elisha had to go out and do the work of Elijah. They were successful in their assignment because they did not allow a spirit of intimidation to overtake them. They did not surrender any of their God-given authority to anyone in Ahab's house. They accomplished what God required of them, delivering an entire nation from Baal worship. Don't make God send someone else to do what He has called you to do! Complete your assignment without feeling intimidated.

The Battle of Words

The Bible tells us another story about intimidation in 1 Samuel 17. It involves David, Goliath and the Philistines:

> And a champion went out from the camp of the Philistines, named Goliath, from Gath, whose height was six cubits and a span. He had a bronze helmet on his head, and he was armed with a coat of mail, and the weight of the coat was five thousand shekels of bronze. And he had bronze armor on his legs and a bronze javelin between his shoulders. Now the staff of his spear was like a weaver's beam, and his iron spearhead weighed six hundred shekels; and a shield-bearer went before him.
>
> 1 Samuel 17:4–7

The first thing intimidating about Goliath was his size. He was huge in stature and was totally covered in heavy armor. That alone can be intimidating, coming up against someone twice your size. Goliath was also shouting threats: "Then he stood and cried out to the armies of Israel, and said to them, 'Why have you come out to line up for battle? Am I not a Philistine, and you the servants of Saul? Choose a man for yourselves, and let him come down to me'" (verse 8). He was trying to win the battle with his words, by making himself sound superior. He was also trying to intimidate the servants of Saul and make them feel lowly, inferior and like victims.

How many times do people do the same thing to us? They cut us down and tell us things that are untrue. We begin to feel bad about ourselves and feel as though we are no good or are unworthy. We give in to intimidation, knowingly or unknowingly, and allow fear to set in. We then end up submitting to people because we don't like confrontation, and the result is that we give them control.

We could take a lesson from Goliath here and try to win the battle with words—but God's words, not ours. I don't mean we want to intimidate people; I mean we can win the battle by warring and praying. We can win the war in the spiritual by speaking out and claiming, by commanding, and by decreeing the Word of God. When we win the war in the spiritual realm, then the war in the natural realm will cease. When the battle is in our mind and that is where intimidation resides, the best way to combat it is with our words. We counterattack by speaking out words, especially God's Word.

Goliath gives us an example of how words intimidate when he tells the Israelite army, "If he is able to fight with me and kill me, then we will be your servants. But if I prevail against him and kill him, then you shall be our servants and serve us" (1 Samuel 17:9). These words were empty promises Goliath did not think he would have to honor. He used his words as a tool to cause fear and intimidation.

How often do another person's words against us cause fear and intimidation? Words spoken against us or toward us paralyze us, and then we don't rise up and fight. Unfortunately, Goliath's intimidating words entered the Israelites' minds and hearts: "And the Philistine said, 'I defy the armies of Israel this day; give me a man, that we may fight together.' When Saul and all Israel heard these words of the Philistine, they were dismayed and greatly afraid" (1 Samuel 17:10–11). Goliath was persistent, too: "And the Philistine drew near and presented himself forty days, morning and evening" (verse 16). Twice a day for forty days, Goliath kept the intimidation coming.

Our enemies are likewise persistent. The devil is persistent. If we were just as persistent, if not more, about capturing every thought and not allowing the lying spirits that feed intimidation to come into our mind, we would win the battle against intimidation.

David heard Goliath's intimidating words: "Then as he talked with them, there was the champion, the Philistine of Gath, Goliath by name, coming up from the armies of the Philistines; and he spoke according to the same words. So David heard them" (verse 23). Goliath was relentless in speaking intimidation, and "all the men of Israel, when they saw the man, fled from him and were dreadfully afraid" (verse 24). The men reacted in intimidation and fear, fleeing not just because of his stature, but also because of his words. The battle was in Goliath's words!

David did not allow intimidation. Instead, he purposed in his heart to take care of Goliath once and for all:

Then David said to Saul, "Let no man's heart fail because of him; your servant will go and fight with this Philistine."

And Saul said to David, "You are not able to go against this Philistine to fight with him; for you are a youth, and he a man of war from his youth."

But David said to Saul, "Your servant used to keep his father's sheep, and when a lion or a bear came and took a lamb out of the flock, I went out after it and struck it, and delivered the lamb from its mouth; and when it arose against me, I caught it by its beard, and struck and killed it. Your servant has killed both lion and bear; and this uncircumcised Philistine will be like one of them, seeing he has defied the armies of the living God." Moreover, David said, "The LORD, who delivered me from the paw of the lion and from the paw of the bear, He will deliver me from the hand of this Philistine."

And Saul said to David, "Go, and the LORD be with you!"

1 Samuel 17:32–37

David had an innocence about him, and a confidence. He had trust and faith that the same God who had delivered him in the past would deliver him in the present and save him in the future.

Remembering God's Actions

Elijah forgot, I think, about how God supernaturally gave him nourishment through the ravens and the widow. He needed to let go of that intimidation and trust that the same God who had saved him in the past would save him in the future.

We, too, need to remember that the God who acted in our past will once again come through for us in our present situation. When we forget what God has done for us in the past, we don't trust that He will take action for us in the future. When we forget the victories of the past, it paralyzes us from acting in the future. Yet "Jesus Christ is the same yesterday, today, and forever" (Hebrews 13:8).

David went into battle with Goliath unprotected in the natural, but with a faith that was supernatural:

> So Saul clothed David with his armor, and he put a bronze helmet on his head; he also clothed him with a coat of mail. David fastened his sword to his armor and tried to walk, for he had not tested them. And David said to Saul, "I cannot walk with these, for I have not tested them." So David took them off.
>
> Then he took his staff in his hand; and he chose for himself five smooth stones from the brook, and put them in a shepherd's bag, in a pouch which he had, and his sling was in his hand. And he drew near to the Philistine.
>
> 1 Samuel 17:38–40

We, too, can have that kind of faith. And the faith to beat intimidation comes from being in God's Word and praying. We cannot allow people to shake us. We need to build up our spiritual armor. Goliath was trying to shake David:

> So the Philistine came, and began drawing near to David, and the man who bore the shield went before him. And when the Philistine looked about and saw David, he disdained him; for he was only a youth, ruddy and good-looking. So the Philistine said to David, "Am I a dog, that you come to me with sticks?" And the Philistine cursed

David by his gods. And the Philistine said to David, "Come to me, and I will give your flesh to the birds of the air and the beasts of the field!"

1 Samuel 17:41–44

David Prophesied Results

David, however, did not take Goliath at his word or allow the giant to intimidate him. Instead, he prophesied that he would be victorious!

> Then David said to the Philistine, "You come to me with a sword, with a spear, and with a javelin. But I come to you in the name of the LORD of hosts, the God of the armies of Israel, whom you have defied. This day the LORD will deliver you into my hand, and I will strike you and take your head from you. And this day I will give the carcasses of the camp of the Philistines to the birds of the air and the wild beasts of the earth, that all the earth may know that there is a God in Israel. Then all this assembly shall know that the LORD does not save with sword and spear; for the battle is the LORD's, and He will give you into our hands."

1 Samuel 17:45–47

David went in the name of the Lord, and we, too, go in His name. When I was being set free from intimidation, I was invited to speak at an event. My overseer did not have a good feeling about it, so he prayed and felt the Lord leading him to accompany me on the trip. When we arrived, we could feel the spirit of intimidation in the atmosphere. Many details were involved, but to summarize, we ended up discovering that we were ministering in a place run by a warlock in disguise. On the first evening, I was not properly equipped to handle the intimidation. I stayed up that night to pray. My overseer and I walked down the hotel hallway, and I kept repeating to myself the good biblical advice he had given me: *I go in Jesus' name* (see 1 Samuel 17:45).

My heavenly Father gave me the battle plan during that night. He told me how to dress, what to preach on, and how to break the cultic cords over these people. I went into that meeting in battle mode! I was not going to allow intimidation to gain control of that meeting and rule the people. The Lord had sent me on assignment to expose the enemy. I wanted the occult exposed and Jesus to be known as the Bridegroom.

I remember some words my overseer delivered to me in that situation: "Preach your way through. Preach the Gospel! It delivers." He also told me, "No intimidation! Be bold! You have Jesus' authority! Walk in it! Own it! Release it!"

I say the same things to you. You don't have to be intimidated. Put on your helmet of faith—or as I call it, your battle cap. I did, literally. I wear fashionable hats, but that evening I put on my battle cap. I did not receive a spirit of intimidation, but of power and love, and I went in there and exposed the truth of God's Word, and people were set free.

Self-Invited Intimidation

Intimidation is a mind game, and most of the time a matter of perception. I remember on one ministry trip I wanted to borrow a storage tote from a friend to take along, but this person wanted to ask her spouse first because she felt intimidated about it. I thought, *I can't believe we need to ask permission to take along something so minor that belongs to both of them.* When I talked to her about it, she realized that in reality her husband wasn't even concerned about it, but she was bringing on herself intimidation rooted in past circumstances.

Another area where we can bring on self-invited intimidation is in our worship. Perhaps you desire to go deeper in your worship or feel led to try new things, but you feel intimidated about what your family, friends or church leaders will think. We allow that intimidation to paralyze us from moving in the realms of the Spirit and going deeper in our worship with the Lord. We must bind and restrict those thoughts that will hinder us from moving into the place the Lord wants to bring us. Our concerns cannot be about what other people will think, or we are being intimidated.

I am a worshiper, and the Lord would say to me during worship, *Kathy, your one act of obedience or disobedience can institute or prevent an altar call or a mighty move of God.* From that point on, I never allowed anything to hold me back. I did what God called me to do, sometimes still wondering, *What are others thinking of me now?* Yet I still took action, even with thoughts like that raging through my mind. I was not going to allow my fear of man to be greater than my fear of God.

Walking Out Your Deliverance

Write yourself some battle notes about conquering intimidation and keep them on your mirror, in your vehicle and in the front of your Bible. Here are some possibilities:

- Take every thought captive.
- Be bold, yet controlled.
- Don't compromise your beliefs.
- Release the authority Christ has given you.
- Flow in the gifts God has given you.
- Go forward, in Jesus' name.

Scriptures on Boldness

Deuteronomy 3:22; 31:6; Joshua 1:9; Psalm 28:1; 34:41; 56:3; 138:3; Isaiah 43:1; 1 Corinthians 16:13

Prayer of Repentance and Forgiveness

Pray this prayer audibly to repent and release forgiveness:

Heavenly Father, I choose to forgive anyone who has made me feel fearful, inferior or intimidated. I forgive anyone who has influenced me toward compromising my beliefs. I am sorry for not standing up and opening my mouth to say something when someone did something in front of me that was wrong.

I break agreement with the spirit of intimidation, and I command it to be cast out of my life.

I ask You, Father, to forgive me for any participation in intimidation, in Jesus' name! Amen!

Spirits to Discern and Cast Out

Ask the Holy Spirit to reveal all the demonic spirits associated with intimidation that you need to cast out. Out loud, command these spirits to leave: "Spirit of _____, go, in Jesus' name!" You may have to do this several times over a period of time. Do it until you feel peace, a release or a spiritual shift. Spirits often associated with intimidation:

Fear, guilt, inferiority, intimidation, insecurity, lying, rejection, mind-binding, mind control, shame

Prayer of Activation

Lord, I receive the Spirit of power and love that Your Word says I have. I have not been given a spirit of fear and intimidation. I receive the boldness of a lion. I refuse to believe anything but Your best for me as I go forth into healing and ministry. I am equipped in every good and perfect thing. Your love for me is great, and I walk in its power. I activate my faith and bring my thoughts and actions into alignment with Your Word. I will not succumb to fear. I will walk in the authority Jesus came to give me, and I will be victorious in all that I set my hand to, in Jesus' name. Amen.

Declarations to Speak Out

Speak out the following faith declarations and spiritual warfare declarations. Bookmark these pages and come back to them as often as necessary to assist you in renewing your mind, transforming your heart and increasing your faith.

Faith Declarations

Make these faith declarations audibly, with power and authority, believing that you will receive them. Speak them out from a position of *I have these*, not *I'm trying to obtain these*. While you transition from intimidation to boldness, read these declarations out regularly to help you grow strong in faith and renew your mind.

- I call forth that I am strong and as bold as a lion.
- I proclaim that my mouth is anointed for the Lord and that I am a spokesperson for His Word.
- I command every intimidation attempt trying to infiltrate me to be bound and restricted from activation, in Jesus' name.
- I am a mighty warrior in God's army, and I have all I need because the Spirit of the Lord lives in me.
- I declare that when fear and intimidation come my way, I will rise up and take my authority.
- I choose to rebuke thoughts of intimidation, fear, anxiety, and fear of what other people think. I serve God my Father, and His thoughts are what are important to me.
- I proclaim that I have all I need to conquer every vain imagination and false scenario through the power of the blood of the Lamb, in Jesus' name.

Spiritual Warfare Declarations

Make these spiritual warfare declarations audibly, with power and authority. When you speak out these declarations, you are taking up your God-given authority to bind and restrict the enemy and counteract future attacks. Declare them repeatedly, until you feel something release in the spiritual atmosphere.

- I bind, restrict and forbid the enemy from infiltrating my thoughts. I will not receive a spirit of intimidation.
- Devil, I cast you down and shut you up; I say you have no power over me. I am bought and paid for with the blood of Christ, and no weapon formed against me will prosper.
- I decree and declare that I have the mind of Christ. He guards my thoughts and keeps them productive and fruitful for the Kingdom of God.
- I call forth every perfect plan for me to walk in righteousness, power and authority to be established now, in Jesus' name.
- I proclaim that no weapon formed against my mind will prosper. I wear the helmet of salvation, which is the helmet of deliverance.
- I decree and declare that I submit all my thoughts to the Word of God, in Jesus' name.

CHAPTER 5

CONTROL

On a scale of 1 to 10, rate each statement below.

1. I have to fix other people's work when I assign them a task, because they don't do it exactly the way I want it completed.
2. I speak certain words to other people in order to achieve the outcome I desire.
3. I often give my children and spouse unsolicited advice, and I have to have input on their decisions.
4. I like everything neat, in order and in its place.
5. I take the ball and roll with it; I don't wait for things to happen naturally.
6. When people ask for advice, I respond immediately, without taking it to prayer.
7. I get off-kilter when things in my day don't go as planned.

In the early years of my marriage, I always needed to have my way. When it was time to pick what restaurant we would eat at, I had to be "highly influential" in the decision. Holidays were supposed to rotate between families, and I did my best to manipulate that schedule as much as I could, to get my way. I had little patience and wanted things done on my timetable. I came from a generational line of controllers, which I did not realize was the root entry point of my control issues until I began the deliverance process.

We are all familiar with control. We know someone who has been in control, has tried to control us, or whose control we have had to submit to. As you read this, however, I ask that you not try to figure out who those people are in your life and point fingers. Instead, examine your heart and allow the Holy Spirit to convict you about yourself. Everyone desires to have a measure of control. If we do our part to reduce the amount of control we exercise over people, we can in exchange release more love and live in unity.

My control issues started as a generational curse, and then I took on my own spirit of control. I can still see the effects of the generational curse of control in my extended family today. Now that I have been delivered, it is easy to see how it destroys relationships and creates dissension in families. I have done my part to root out the control and teach my young adult children how to release what they inherited from me. It has to start with someone in the family line rooting control out and stopping it, and today I am asking if you will consider allowing this process to start with you.

Control is not easy to give up. It makes an appearance in many different ways. Whenever I thought I was delivered of it, the Holy Spirit would bring forth another level. It is not always easy to discover our faults, or areas of life where we don't want to let go. If you think about it, however, being controlling really stresses you out. You are always working overtime to micromanage everyone and everything to get the results to come out in your favor. It is tiring. It is sin. It needs to be removed from our lives and the lives of those we love. When we look at many of the mishaps in the world, we can see they are triggered by control. How many things would have turned out differently in your life if control had not been the disrupter?

Control goes undiscovered because it masquerades in a person who is an organizer and leader. It can be undetected in a family member because our view of family is that one person is in charge and runs the family well, organizing events, keeping the family together and working out the details. That person is usually a controller. We have to define what is normal to do because it is our responsibility, versus when we have gone overboard and our control has become detrimental. Defining that is crucial in finding a balance in our lives.

The Bible's story of Jezebel and Ahab illustrates control. Jezebel displayed a powerful manifestation of a controlling spirit. She was mean, vindictive and manipulating. It was obvious that she held onto control and power. Ahab was more subtle about his control. He was the quiet, controlling manipulator behind Jezebel.

In 1 Kings 16:31, Ahab marries Jezebel, a zealous worshiper of Baal, and she takes him along to worship her god—a step in her control. In 1 Kings 18:4, Jezebel murders the prophets of the Lord, except for 100 who were hidden. Her actions show how complacent Ahab was, allowing his wife to be in control and make decisions. In 1 Kings 21, Ahab wanted his neighbor's vineyard, but the neighbor did not want to give it up. Ahab acts like a little kid, whining and refusing to eat. When Jezebel sees this, she uses her manipulation and control to get this neighbor killed. Her husband then gets the vineyard, and it makes her happy. Controlling people have a need to get their own way, even if they don't know it.

In Judges 16:4–22, we see in Delilah another illustration of a controller. She was the queen of manipulation, which she used to control Samson. She was trying to find out where his strength came from, because she wanted all the money the Philistines promised her if she would help them capture him. First, she tries to manipulate him with her anger: "Look, you have mocked me and told me lies!" (verse 10). Then she tries to manipulate him with her whining: "How can you say, 'I love you,' when your heart is not with me?" (verse 15). Then she tries nagging and pestering: "And it came to pass when she pestered him daily with her words and pressed him, so that his soul was vexed to death, that he told her all his heart" (verse 16).

Manipulation and control exist together. You cannot have one without the other. Delilah and Jezebel both used manipulation to get what they wanted. In order to be delivered from control, we must be educated on what spirits work together to assist the strongman we are trying to root out. The Lord gave me a vision once of control being like the body of a spider. Control is the body, but each leg is a different spirit holding the body together and keeping the body in operation. In our lives, we need to cut off the legs of the spider—the emotional issues and demonic roots that are supporting the body. We need to destroy control's support system, and then the body, the main spirit of control, will fail.

Rebellion

Rebellion is one of the strongest hidden operations behind the spirit of control. When we rebel, we are controlling a situation. It can go in two different ways: We can rebel against a boss, leader, spouse or minister and the instructions they desire us to follow, or we can rebel against God by deliberately not obeying an instruction He releases to us. When you don't do what you know you should, you are saying, *I know better than the other person (or better than God). I'm not going to listen to them (or to God); I'm going to do things my own way because my way is better, and I know best.*

When we think of rebellion, we like to relate it to teenagers being rebellious, or to wayward children or someone defiling authority. We think of it as arguing against another's opinion and direction. Rebellion comes in different forms, however, and follows us into our adulthood and into our relationship with our heavenly Father. Webster defines it as "opposition to one in authority or dominance."[1]

Betrayal, hurt and offense lead to rebellion. I was once in rebellion in a ministry relationship. I had been in leadership for years and had experienced my fair share of church hurts, as I am sure you may have. All of these hurts, betrayals and offenses built up a stronghold of rebellion in my life. I knew I had been hurt, but I was unaware of the rebellious spirit that had entered as a result. When you get hurt so many times, you put up self-protective walls and make vows such as *I'll never allow anyone to hurt me again.* Even though those thoughts did not enter my mind and I made no such vows consciously, my actions and the words I used in ministry revealed them.

When I got out on my own, I was proud of establishing my ministry without assistance. Then God introduced me to a holy man of God. Meeting this man just the first time, he had a huge impact on me because of his humility and intimacy with the Father. I declared for months afterward, "I will have this man as my spiritual father."

God answered my prayer six short months later, sending me this mentor and overseer in the ministry who was a wonderful gift and who would love me unconditionally. Yet I did not always see him as a gift. Even though I wanted him in my life and he was an answer to prayer, subconsciously over a period of time I tried to do everything I could to sabotage our relationship. I would be nice one minute and rebel the next.

Why did I rebel against something I had wanted and declared my belief for? Because I had been hurt several times by church leaders, so I figured that if I acted as though I could remain in control of the relationship, I could prevent this man from hurting me. I was trying to push him away before any hurt could happen. Rebellion wants to take control of our soul (our mind, will and emotions) so that

1. *Merriam-Webster* online, s.v. "Rebellion," https://www.merriam-webster.com/dictionary/rebellion.

we insist on doing things our own way. The rebellion in me finally did push away the good gift God had given me in this overseer. I thought I was healed, but I wasn't. I thought I was right. I wanted to be in control. I thought he was wrong, because rebellion does not want to be told what to do. For three years I pushed away God's gift, the very thing I had cried out in prayer for.

Thankfully, on the first day of Teshuvah one year, I started a fast. Teshuvah is part of the Jewish High Holidays, a time of repentance and turning back to God that we Christians can observe as part of our Jewish heritage. When we are rebellious, we don't want anyone watching out for our soul because we feel we can do it ourselves, yet Hebrews13:17 says it all: "Obey those who rule over you, and be submissive, for they watch out for your souls." That is powerful! Obey and be in submission to them, because such leaders watch out for our souls. It is so true. I needed someone to watch out for my soul. I needed accountability. The Holy Spirit convicted me that I needed this overseer back in my life. This man now makes sure I keep my face before the Father in the secret place. He encourages me constantly to sing, dance, worship, declare, pray, fast, study the Word and stay before the face of God for hours on end.

Rejection

In the case of my overseer, I was trying to reject him before he had the chance to reject me. By doing this, I was in control of my feelings and emotions. If I could set up safeguards, shut myself down to him when I wanted to and not answer his questions, then he could not reject me.

Does this sound like any of the feelings or thoughts that have passed through your mind? Rejection makes us push people away instead of allowing them in. I did that with my overseer. I cried in utter shock and amazement at the goodness of God the day I sat across from him at a table and he asked me, "What do you want? What have you been asking the Lord for?"

I said, "I have only asked one thing of the Father—that He would make you my spiritual father."

When he replied, "I receive you and your ministry," the presence of God came upon us so strongly. The first deliverance conference my overseer and I did together was amazing. Witches were delivered, people were changed, lives were transformed. Even though our relationship was young, we ministered well and tag-teamed together. Each of the three nights that first time, I would go back to my hotel room and weep into the night at the goodness of God and how He had orchestrated this relationship.

Yet over the course of the next year, the rebellion and rejection in me also wanted to reject him before he could reject me, and those played with my mind, attempting to invade and sabotage our relationship. That is how demonic spirits, vain imaginations and past emotional soul wounds manifest when we have not received deliverance.

What are you subconsciously sabotaging and throwing away that God is trying to give you? The Bible says, "Do not harden your hearts, as in the rebellion" (Psalm 95:8). Rebellion causes hardness of heart. When you co-labor with rebellion, you shut down your feelings, withdraw and put up self-protective walls. You shove your problems down deep inside your soul so you don't have to deal with them. If you don't deal with them, then you don't have to feel. It is easier for some people not to feel than to deal with their emotions.

Pride

Pride and rejection are co-laborers of rebellion. When Satan exalted himself and allowed pride to enter and manifest, he became rebellious toward God. "Pride goes before destruction, and a haughty spirit before a fall" (Proverbs 16:18). Satan's rebellion and pride caused a great fall.

If we are not careful, the same thing can happen to us. Pride can attack our life that way, too. Pride says, *I know I'm right and you're wrong.* Pride says, *It's my way or the highway.* These statements are rebellion and pride talking hand in hand. We cannot cast a spirit of pride out knowing that rebellion is feeding it, and vice versa. It is imperative to know what spirits interact together. Then when we are receiving our healing and casting out demons, we can root out everything and leave no remnant behind.

Pride and control are linked to attention. When people speak pridefully and manifest control, whether nicely or in an obnoxious, defiant way, they are receiving attention, even if it is unhealthy attention. Control says, *Look at me. I'm in control, and people listen to me.* People never have pride without attention seeking being attached to it. Pride is all about the attention they can get and how they can exalt themselves.

The concerning part with control and pride issues is that when both are present, people with pride don't see that they have pride issues, and people with control don't see that they have control issues. They think everyone else is wrong and they are right. Before they will change, we often have to rely on their surrender to the Holy Spirit's conviction in their lives to reveal to them that they are operating in these two spirits.

As we want more of God and cry out to the Father for cleansing, He will reveal these things to us in our prayer time or through a mentor. We must be willing to acknowledge any of our issues and bring forth change from the revelation we receive.

No Flesh

Disobedience toward the instruction of God and conviction from the Holy Spirit is rebellion. "How?" you may ask. Let's use food addictions as an example. The Holy Spirit begins to instruct you about what to eat and what not to eat. He gives you a list of things not to put in your mouth. Still, you eat them. As you walk by the cookie jar, grab a cookie and bring it to your mouth, He convicts you and says, *Put it back*. You justify it instead, saying, *It's already in my hand*, and you eat it.

Or we rebel against God when He instructs us to spend an hour in prayer, and we only spend twenty minutes. We think that is good enough. But who are we to disagree with the directions God has given us? When we don't obey what He has told us to do, we are saying that we know better than He does.

One of my favorite sayings is "No flesh," or "Flesh is not an option." Rebellion requires us to cast down our flesh. We rebel because we want what we want when we want it. We want to do things our way, satisfy the flesh and not be told what to do. We either think we know best, or we don't feel like doing it another way. Our flesh wants. Our flesh craves. Our flesh desires. Yet we are spirit people. Our flesh will die and decay in a grave someday. It is not important to satisfy our flesh; what is important is that we are in the perfect will of our Father.

Sarai gave in to her flesh out of rebellion when she wanted a child, and then she regretted it. She was tired of waiting, so she gave her handmaiden to her husband (see Genesis 16:1–6). We will regret the actions we take in rebellion. In Sarai's case, the rebellious deed could not be undone. A child was born, and she had to live with that for the rest of her life. By acting out in rebellion, we also can make mistakes in our flesh that we have to deal with for the rest of our lives. That's why I encourage my team to bind their flesh. We have a sign in our ministry center that says, "No Flesh." Our flesh can and does get us into trouble.

Solomon rebelled against God when he married against His commands in 1 Kings 11:1–11. That rebellion cost Solomon a lot. He left his love of God and followed false idols, and he lost his kingdom. His rebellion is related to what people experience today. I minister to people who are unhappily married. My question to them is, "Did you pray about marrying this person?"

When our flesh or emotions get involved, we can ignore God's warning signs and want what we want, not even considering praying about such decisions. My daughter, Lauren, and I pray about most things. Decisions people would just make themselves, we pray about. It may seem overboard to some, but God can and does protect you from things when you allow Him to orchestrate the pathway of your life and make decisions on your behalf.

Discerning Your Path to Freedom

Ezekiel 12:2 says, "Son of man, you dwell in the midst of a rebellious house, which has eyes to see but does not see, and ears to hear but does not hear; for they are a rebellious house." Rebellious people don't want to hear what God has to say. They subconsciously close off their spiritual ears, although they may pray and think they are hearing from Him. Really, it is their own thoughts they are hearing.

Self-evaluate to prevent that kind of rebellion by asking yourself, *Is this how God would talk to me, or is this how I would speak to myself?* By using that comparison, you can often see that it is your own thoughts in your mind speaking to you, instead of God depositing an answer into your spirit.[2]

Rebellious people don't want to hear from God because they don't want to do what they think He will "make" them do. They perceive God's instruction as forcing them to do something against their will. We discover more about such rebellion in the book of Isaiah: "That this is a rebellious people, lying children, children who will not hear the law of the LORD; who say to the seers, 'Do not see,' and to the prophets, 'Do not prophesy to us right things; speak to us smooth things, prophesy deceits'" (Isaiah 30:9–10).

I was astounded the first time I really read this! Rebellious people would really ask to be prophesied deceitful things, the smooth things, instead of what the will of God and word of the Lord is for them? Every time we speak a word, it is prophetically assigned. God has given us authority, and when we speak out, we

---

2. In my book *Who Is Speaking?* (CreateSpace, 2018), you can discover more about the difference between the sources you hear from.

activate the spiritual realm. Our words have power and get results; things happen and shift in the spiritual realm when we declare things out and speak audibly.[3] So we should only be speaking the will and Word of God.

In God's eyes, rebellion is in the same category as witchcraft: "For rebellion is as the sin of witchcraft, and stubbornness is as iniquity and idolatry" (1 Samuel 15:23). I don't think that if you are reading this book, you would consciously be engaging in witchcraft. But as we read here, God considers it the same as witchcraft when we are rebellious.

What about Saul's rebellion in 1 Samuel 16:14–23, which caused a demon to enter him? Sin and rebellion are an open door for an evil spirit. We have all sinned, and now is the time to cast out any spirits associated with our sins. Sin opens the door for the enemy, providing him what I call a legal right. When we knowingly sin and rebel, the enemy has a legal right to infiltrate our soul. One of the reasons deliverance ministry can be challenging is because we have partnered with sin and have allowed the enemy those legal rights. Removing what I have been calling the "root cause" means removing the sin that gave demonic forces the legal right to enter and manifest as a stronghold in our lives.

We need to pursue healing that will lead us to freedom. Inviting the Holy Spirit to come in and convict us is one way to expose and root out what inhibits us from God. We also need to self-examine consistently and conduct self-deliverance as a way to expose and root out those things. We want to be clean vessels that are purified, useful and effective for the Kingdom. We don't want to be full of sin and things that do not glorify God. Ask the Holy Spirit, "Create in me a clean heart" (Psalm 51:10). Tell Him, "Search me, O God, and know my heart; try me, and know my anxieties; and see if there is any wicked way in me, and lead me in the way everlasting" (Psalm 139:23–24).

---

3. See my book *Speak Out* (Creation House, 2017) for more on the power of our words.

Rebellion and several other demonic spirits feed the control in our lives. A controlling spirit causes much damage and ruins relationships. Jezebel, the name of a strongman spirit of control, is a destroyer. The God we serve can deliver anyone who will repent, change and turn from his or her ways. While we may not like what we see in ourselves when we self-examine, we need to remember that what we are seeing is not the spirit person God created us to be. It is a demonic spirit operating through the area of our soul and in our behavioral patterns, habits and attitudes. We can change. The question is, Will we change? Separate the person, *you*, from the principality manipulating you. Don't condemn yourself as you receive this information. Use this knowledge to lead you to and through deliverance.

Inheriting Control

Control usually begins as a generational spirit that we inherit. The challenge is that it becomes the "normal" us. We take on the habits we are raised around as normal. We need to remove faulty perceptions of the norm that have been instilled in us. But controlling people often don't want to be corrected or proven wrong. They always want to give the appearance that they are right, so they will justify or correct whatever anyone else has said. Often, they will interrupt and attempt to control a conversation so that they can jump in and make their point. Or they will keep giving input even when a conversation is done, just to ensure that their point is heard.

Control from our childhood could still be manifesting over us today. We are taught to be controlling through control being exercised over us. Is there something a parent or grandparent said or did that you still think about today? I was always strongly cautioned about driving in the snow, even advised against it. I would try to stay off snowy roads because I would remember those constant warnings. I had it drilled in my mind so much that as an adult, I had to overcome the fear of it. Even though I lived on my own,

I was still allowing those thoughts and words from my childhood to control me. This was an area in which I needed deliverance.

I remember the day God was dealing with me about fear and control, and it began to snow. He instructed me to get into my vehicle, drive to the store and purchase a sign that said *freedom*, which I did. Since then, I have been able to drive in snowy conditions without fear, and I have even driven in hazardous conditions whenever God has told me to go! As a mom, I have also made a conscious effort not to control my kids by passing on to them the same fear of driving in winter that was passed on to me.

You have to desire freedom in order to give up control and allow the Holy Spirit to lead you through the process of deliverance. I recently heard a couple of young adults speak out about themselves, "I like being in control. I'm a control freak." This is not a good thing! Obviously, they are not ready to pursue their freedom. Even though they are actually aware that there is a generational curse of control in their families, they don't know that they can be delivered. They also have established their own spirit of control because they have co-labored with it and welcomed it. So two spirits of control are in evidence here. One is a generational spirit of control, and the second is a spirit of control. You can have more than one spirit of the same thing. In deliverance ministry, these are each called out individually as "generational spirit of control, I command you to get out, in Jesus' name," and "spirit of control, I command you to get out, in Jesus' name." When dealing with spirits, we need to be discerning and seek the Holy Spirit about whether there is simply a spirit present from our own sin, or whether there is more than one—a spirit from our sin, and also a spirit from the sin of our generational line.

People who desire freedom must recognize that they are operating under a spirit of control. It is difficult to hear that you are a controlling person. It makes it sound as if you are not very nice. In my experience, unless a controlling person is a mature believer and is desperately and diligently seeking God for freedom in all areas, it is difficult to be delivered. Control wants to hold you back from the fullness of God and keep you bound. It manifests in so many ways that we often don't recognize it in ourselves, and when someone mentions it to us, we get offended and prideful, and we dismiss the thought that it is manifesting in our life. When we surrender to God and are open to what the Spirit of the Lord is telling us, however, then we can be correctable and receive the deliverance He wants to give us.

Destroying patterns and habits of control requires a conscious effort on our part. You can cast out a demon of control, but you still have to unlearn everything you learned over the years about being controlling. Examine yourself and ask, *How am I manifesting control?* Allow the Holy Spirit to reveal where you might be controlling. Reflect on and repent of where you have been operating in this spirit. Allow the Holy Spirit to convict you about where you need to change, and ask Him for divine strategies to bring that change forth.

Operating with control over a long period of time can be difficult to release. Yet as we repent and allow the Holy Spirit to convict us, we can slowly begin to give up the behavioral pattern of control and walk out the fullness of our freedom.

Walking Out Your Deliverance

To walk out of control requires taking every thought captive and submitting it to the obedience of Christ (see 2 Corinthians 10:4–5). That means when a thought comes that you want to act on in a certain way, you need to ask yourself, *Would Jesus act this way?* You need to take every thought, every action and every word to prayer. Our life is not our own; it belongs to the One on the throne. We should be in constant submission to Him.

Scriptures on Submission

Jeremiah 17:10; Malachi 2:10; Romans 13:1; 1 Corinthians 1:10; Titus 3:1; James 4:7

Prayer of Forgiveness and Repentance

Pray this prayer audibly to repent and release forgiveness:

God, I ask for Your forgiveness. Help me be submissive. Holy Spirit, convict me when I am acting out in behavior that does not please my Father. Teach me to submit, obey, persevere, cooperate and act in a manner pleasing to God. Forgive me for the times I have acted out in rebellion, control and manipulation. I thank You, God, for Your forgiveness, and I forgive myself.

Right now, in the name of Jesus, I break agreement with the spirits of Jezebel, and control and manipulation. I command you to deactivate now!

I thank You, God, for Your forgiveness, and I forgive myself.

I break all curses that I may have put on another person, and I release the demonic realm of their assignment against me and other people.

In the name of Jesus, I choose today to forgive those who have acted against me by being controlling and manipulative. I recognize that I have been warring against a principality and not a person. I forgive the person who has acted out against me, as I now know my battle is with the principality. I accept the atonement of forgiveness that Jesus purchased for me, and I extend that forgiveness to others, in Jesus' name. Amen!

Spirits to Discern and Cast Out

Ask the Holy Spirit to reveal all the demonic spirits associated with control that you need to cast out. Out loud, command these spirits to leave: "Spirit of _____, go, in Jesus' name!" You may have to do this several times over a period of time. Do it until you feel peace, a release or a spiritual shift. Spirits often associated with control:

Anger, attention, bitterness, control, deception, disobedience, generational control, fear, fear of rejection, haughtiness, Jezebel, intimidation, lying, manipulation, murder, pride, rebellion, rejection, striving, stubbornness, superiority, temper, unforgiveness, violence, witchcraft

Prayer of Activation

Father, I thank You that rebellion has been rooted out and that I have a submitted soul. Father, help my soul—my mind, will and emotions—come into alignment with Your divine plan for my life.

When things don't go my way, or when I feel the need to rebel and control, Holy Spirit, convict me, teach me and instruct me. I submit to Your divine plan for my life.

Father, help me realize that I don't need to be controlling. Help me be submissive and not rebellious. I desire You to consume me. Help me be so full of Your love that I never desire to have control or manipulate to get my own way. Father, shower me with Your love, and help me see others as more important than myself, in Jesus' name. Amen!

Declarations to Speak Out

Speak out the following faith declarations and spiritual warfare declarations. Bookmark these pages and come back to them as often as necessary to assist you in renewing your mind, transforming your heart and increasing your faith.

Faith Declarations

Make these faith declarations audibly, with power and authority, believing that you will receive them. Speak them out from a position of *I have these*, not *I'm trying to obtain these*. Read these declarations out regularly to help you grow strong in faith and renew your mind.

- I cancel every generational assignment of control on my life.
- I release offenders from their offenses against me. I forgive them for controlling me.
- I speak and declare that I am emotionally healed from the need to rebel.
- I call forth an attitude of cooperation and love. Father, allow me to be an extension of Your love.
- I will yield to the Holy Spirit and pray when I feel the need to control.
- I will follow the biblical principles of submitting to those in authority over me.
- I will watch my words and decisions so as not to exude manipulation, control and rebellion subconsciously.
- I will trust God at all times and for my life, even when I cannot see the outcome. I will live by faith and not by sight, in Jesus' name.

Spiritual Warfare Declarations

Make these spiritual warfare declarations audibly, with power and authority. When you speak out these declarations, you are taking up your God-given authority to bind and restrict the enemy and counteract future attacks. Declare them repeatedly, until you feel something release in the spiritual atmosphere.

- I speak against every principality operating against me, and I say you are abolished of your assignment, in Jesus' name.
- I rebuke and renounce every thought that attacks my soul to tell me I must have my way.
- I renounce and give up the need to control situations.
- I bind and restrict my flesh and say you will not act out in ungodly ways.
- I cancel every generational curse against my life, and I bind the devourer from activating on past curses, in Jesus' name.

- I will pray before I speak, making sure my thoughts and intentions are pure.
- Every Jezebel spirit coming against my destiny, you are relinquished of your assignment now, in Jesus' name.
- I choose to forgive; therefore, I am no longer bound in rebellion.
- I speak out that I fear the Lord; therefore, I will not act unwisely.
- I break off and cancel all demonic atmospheres (weights and heaviness) hovering over my life like a cloud, in Jesus' name.

CHAPTER 6

PRIDE

Self-Assessment—Spirit of Pride

On a scale of 1 to 10, rate each statement below.

1. I like to try to figure things out for myself, and I only ask for help as a last resort.
2. I often share my story when others are talking about something I have experienced.
3. I don't think I have a pride issue.
4. I feel my experiences can override another person's knowledge and opinion.
5. I have to look my best at all times.
6. I want people to notice and acknowledge me.
7. I often wonder what other people think of me.

I remember my husband telling me for years that I had an issue with pride. I would respond with, "No, I don't."

I usually take something someone says and stew on it for a while. I mull it over, ponder it and see if I can discover any truth to it. In this case, I did not even consider it. We often don't want to receive from those closest to us, but sometimes they see things in us that we don't see in ourselves. Years later, when I was with my overseer, he also said I had a pride issue. He would really get on me about it some days, enough to make me pay attention.

The challenge was that I did not manifest pride the same way as another person might. I was a speaker and was running a successful ministry, but I never once thought, *Look at me, I'm on stage, I'm all that*. Thoughts of self-exaltation like that never even entered my mind. But pride has many faces and characteristics. How one person's pride manifests might not be how your pride manifests, yet we all have some measure of pridefulness. My overseer dug into this issue enough that I had to look more closely inside myself and root out what God wanted to extinguish in my life. After putting myself on the Lord's altar, I discovered I was prideful.

Pride is one of the most easily identifiable spirits to see on someone else, even though it is blinding to the person carrying it. People wear pride on their sleeve. Wanting to go into a meeting to impress someone is prideful. When we approach people and try to impress them or make them notice us, they can easily identify our pridefulness. Pride comes with arrogance and self-confidence, instead of "God confidence." Pride can be attached to an unhealthy need and desire for attention.

What if, like me, you say you have no pridefulness? What if you have never even considered the fact that you are prideful? Isn't that pride? What if you don't want to ask for help or assistance, or what if you feel someone else is prideful? Did you ever examine yourself for a pride issue? When we deny being prideful, it can be an evil spirit in operation that is driving us to refuse to even consider whether or not we have issues with pride.

Pride Is Self-Focused

Lucifer took his eyes off everything around him and focused on himself. We get into trouble when we take our eyes off others and place the focus on ourselves. People can see the pride in us, and most people don't want to be around a prideful person. Pride is a ministry killer and a relationship stealer.

People with pride talk a lot and put the focus on their situation and whatever they are going through. When you converse with them, you will repeatedly hear the word "*I.*" This is because pride is blinding. People with pridefulness don't see that they have it, and they are therefore unaware that they are constantly talking about themselves.

We all have some level of pride; to dismiss this would be a lie. People take pride in the clothes they wear, the home they live in or the career they choose. Instead of being prideful over our material possessions, we need to take the things we are proud of and enjoy having and use them for the glory of the Kingdom of God. When we use them to glorify the Lord, we have just transitioned from being prideful about them to walking in humility.

When Satan turned his thoughts from God to himself, pride took hold. He entertained thoughts of pride and self-exaltation instead of rejecting those thoughts. He should have taken those thoughts captive, smashed them down and dismissed them. Instead, he lingered on them long enough for pride to enter. In Isaiah 14 and Ezekiel 28, we learn how Satan did not take hold of his thoughts, and as a result desired to exalt himself above God.

We, too, linger on thoughts we should not have, and as a result we allow pride to enter. We entertain thoughts such as *I have a physically fit body, I know the Word of God better than others,* or *I'm that person of influence's close friend.* We must not allow such thoughts to captivate us—not even for one minute! When thoughts that can result in pridefulness attempt to snare me, I just picture a gavel in my mind. I smash the thoughts with the gavel and throw them out of my mind. It was Satan's thoughts that took him out, and it is thoughts like these that Satan will use to take us out if we don't capture them.

Pride Changes Our Thinking

People with pride issues think differently because pride changes their thinking. For example, when a person is consumed with pride, the words another person speaks are often misconstrued. Pride's main hazard is twisting communication, which damages relationships. People with pride issues hear the words spoken to them, but they often disregard those words. Instead of listening closely, they incorrectly perceive that the speaker has motives different from his or her words, so they dismiss the words or become offended by them, thinking the person is all about himself or herself.

It makes no difference how clearly something is explained, prideful people hear it differently than others. In their mind, they completely substitute the words in a sentence with something else. The speaker can say, "I'm going to the store to buy a jar of jelly," but the prideful person will hear, "I don't like this kind of jelly; I'm going to buy a brand I like better." In more extreme cases of pride, whole topics can be substituted. Instead of hearing something about jelly, the prideful person could hear something about pizza. The level of misunderstanding can coincide with the level of pride a person is manifesting.

Pride, anger and rejection can exist together inside a person's soul. This damages and ruins relationships because not only will prideful people hear things incorrectly; whatever they incorrectly perceive can also make them feel angry or rejected. Often, what they really think they hear is the message "you don't care about me."

We have all had conversations with people who interpret something differently than what we said. Is there a person in your life who misunderstands you? No matter how hard you try to clarify your thoughts and opinions and get the person to listen to you, he or she does not seem to hear what you are saying? That is pridefulness in action.

People who experience pride issues are often unteachable. The spirit of superiority prevents them from being taught by others and from receiving correction. Are you good at receiving correction, or does it irritate you? Pride tells us we are right and everyone else is wrong. You feel like the world is out to get you. The challenge of being bound with a demonic spirit is that most of the time, we don't know we are bound by it until we are free of it. We don't know because when we are truly bound, the demonic spirit lies to us. It speaks to us in our mind and inserts thoughts such as *you are better than this*, *they're wrong*, or *they're lying to you*. These are not our own thoughts. These are thoughts the enemy attacks our mind with, in order to bind us.

Internal and External Characteristics

We can discern pride issues through both the internal and external characteristics we find in people who have issues with it. The following internal manifestations arise out of some character flaws associated with pridefulness:

- Prideful people seldom budge in their opinions and beliefs.
- They think others are looking at them and admiring their physical appearance.
- They are disobedient to God's instructions and are self-reliant instead of God-dependent.
- They are easily irritated by others. Irritation is a spirit that accompanies pride.

- They have little tolerance for the ignorance they perceive others to have. They don't know how to extend grace, acceptance and forgiveness.
- They walk into a room and demand attention, or insist that people notice them. They give off a feeling of *Did you see me? Did you see that I just walked into the room and I'm all that, and I need your attention?*

Prideful people display external character flaws as well. When conversing with them, we may see some of the following signs that are the external manifestations of this spirit:

- Prideful people have an independent spirit. They think they can do things themselves and don't need interference.
- They live a life of prayerlessness; they lack a prayer life.
- They are snobbish.
- They are selective of friends.
- They fail to admit their mistakes.
- They rebel against authority.
- They demand special treatment.
- They have an unteachable spirit, thinking they have arrived.
- They are given to exaggeration, wanting to appear as more than they are.

Ask the Holy Spirit to search your heart and reveal to you whether or not you exhibit any of these and need to seek repentance and deliverance in this area of pridefulness.

Attention Seeking and Pride

Attention seeking co-labors with pride. People with pride issues often have an unhealthy longing for attention, and pride and attention often manifest together. Seeking unhealthy attention can come in different forms. People with this yearning might act out or behave in a way that says *look at me* or *feel sorry for me*. In order to educate you further and help you understand how attention interacts with pride, here are some common ways people who are attention seekers behave:

- A child gets hurt. There are normal emotions children experience when they get hurt emotionally or physically, but this child's attention seeking carries on past expelling the emotion or pain.

- An adult feels physical pain. Adults will not necessarily manifest attention through the words they speak. They will walk into a room and hold the part of their body that hurts, and gently rub it. In essence, they are seeking attention by saying with their actions, *Ask me what's wrong. Don't you see I'm grabbing and rubbing part of my body?*

- A person's countenance changes. Someone will come into a room, a meeting or a group gathering with a sad or depressed look on his or her face. That person may have a genuine problem, but instead of coming out and saying, "Can you pray for me? Something is attacking me," he or she will go around moping until someone else asks what is wrong. The challenge with this spirit of attention is that it distracts from the purposes of a meeting or the things that need to be done. This spirit can also co-labor with a victim mentality, which will we discuss more in chapter 10 on victim and poverty mentalities.

- A person acts differently when new people are around. Someone with an unhealthy longing for attention may say something louder than usual, or may act out with exaggerated body movements to get attention, in essence saying, *Look at me! Notice me!*

Casting down thoughts that go with an unusual desire to have the attention focused on you comes by knowing who you are in Christ. Christ accepts you! Jesus loves you! As you become secure in your walk with the Lord, you won't care what other human beings think. As you know who you are in Christ, you will know that you can have His attentions, and that is what matters.

The Lord is always with us in each and every moment and is ready to listen with His ears wide open. He is attentive to us. We should not need to show off or act out to get affirmation from people, when the Lord has already affirmed us.

Humility Overcomes Pride

Humility is the key to overcoming pride. Humility does not come naturally, however. When we search Scripture, we find the phrase *put on* several times. We read that we are to put on love, put on Christ, and put on the armor of God (see 1 Thessalonians 5:8; Romans 13:14; Ephesians 6:11). We must also put on humility and learn to walk in it. It is not putting on a face that says, *Here I am, acting lowly and humble.* It is genuinely experiencing the humility that is part of Christ's character. We are made in His image. Our spirit man therefore has the ability to be humble. If we can bind our flesh and our soul from taking over in pride, we can walk this out more effectively by pulling on our spirit man.

Humility is being loving toward others and caring about their needs. This is difficult for someone who always wants attention. People with pride issues don't know how to think of someone else as more important than they are, because they think they are the most important. Getting free of this involves a mind transformation. It is laying ourselves aside in order to invest in the lives of others.

Humility is recognizing that everything is God's and comes from Him and should go back to Him. Humility is recognizing that we can do nothing without Him. He is our healer, deliverer and sustainer. Humility is learning that we were created to love God and love people, and to serve God and serve people. It truly is walking in the Spirit and being in constant communication with our Lord.

Years ago, I met a man on whom I could feel the glory of God. I said to him, "You are a holy man of God."

He replied, "No, I am a humble man of God."

There is a difference between holy and humble. Holy is saying, "Yes, I'm holy." It is putting the attention back on us. Humble is saying, "What you're feeling is the Spirit of the Lord within me, and I give the credit to God."

The simple, humble response of this man set me on a quest for true humility. If I told you about this man and his credentials, influence, wealth and the famous people he knows, you would be surprised that he has been able to remain humble through it all. He loves the Lord more than all the other things and people, and that has kept him in a place of humility.

Receiving Compliments and Gifts

One area in which pride and humility can be misconstrued is when we receive a compliment or accept a gift. How do you receive affirmation for a job well done without allowing it to go to your head? Giving God the glory and pointing it back toward Christ is key. You can say something like, "Thanks, but the Lord gave me the gift and wisdom to accomplish this."

When we receive compliments such as "you played the piano beautifully" or "you preached a powerful message," people are commenting on how well we have done something. Sometimes when we then try to give the glory back to God, they will respond with, "Yes, but you were obedient." In those situations, we can simply respond with a gentle, polite thank-you and then once again bring glory back to the Lord by saying, "I was obedient, but that's what the Bible teaches us to be," or "I was obedient, but Jesus was obedient to the cross, so the least I can do is be obedient to what He has called me to."

I don't believe we need to hang our head low or act shy when we receive a compliment. We do have to be cautious, however, that we don't shout out a big "*YES, I did great!*" Even simply keeping our face attentive, with a gentle nod and a subtle thank-you, is an appropriate way to keep ourselves in check and not act out in pride.

Receiving gifts and blessings can also give rise to prideful moments. When a person gives us a gift, he or she usually wants to see us open it. I believe this is a time when we should show emotion. It is okay to get excited, because the giver usually wants to know that we are going to enjoy the gift. It is what we do afterward with that gift or blessing that can catch us in pridefulness. We often want to say, "Look what God just did for me!" And then we want to post it on social media or tell our friends about it. These actions may be genuine, but they may also be prideful. I do believe it is good to share testimonies of what we have received, as long as we do it for the glory of the Kingdom.

I once received a very nice, newer low-mileage Dodge Charger for free. Through prayer and a series of events, the Lord affirmed that I could declare out and claim a Dodge Charger.[1] I claimed and decreed for three years, and the manifestation of my Dodge Charger then came. Now I tell everyone, "That's not my car; it's your car. It's a testimony so you will know the power of believing in God and praying and declaring out what He instructs you to."

My daughter drove my car every day for nine months after I received it, because she did not have a vehicle. My son, in fact, drove it as I was writing this book, at which time I have had this car for four years. It is a silver custom Dodge Charger with decals, custom tires, custom rims, a spoiler and other things that get noticed. The kids can't drive it anywhere without someone commenting on it. The one condition I put on letting them drive

1. See my book *Speak Out* (Creation Space, 2017) for the full story about the car, and for more about the power of praying audibly.

it is that when someone says, "Nice car," they respond with, "God gave my mom that car for free."

Not a day goes by that I do not give glory to God for that car and the blessing it is, and for the testimony it has become to praying audibly. I can't say there has never been a raging, prideful thought that travels through my mind when I am driving it, or when I see people looking out of the corner of their eye to admire it. But in those rare moments, I instantly capture the thought and remember that I would not have the car at all without the Lord.

Walking Out Your Deliverance

To move forward in walking out of pridefulness, be diligent in casting down every thought that does not line up to the Word of God. Repent and ask the Holy Spirit to send you conviction about your words, actions and attitudes. Diligently seek the Lord and His characteristics. Continue in prayer daily, asking God to reveal the condition of your heart to you for assessment and correction.

Scriptures on Humility

Psalm 18:27; 25:9; 34:2; 69:32; 147:6; Proverbs 11:2; 16:19; 29:23; James 4:10; 1 Peter 5:6

Prayer of Repentance and Forgiveness

Pray this prayer audibly to repent and release forgiveness:

Heavenly Father, please forgive me for being prideful. Forgive me when I have exalted myself, or my position, and forgive me for the hurt I have caused other people due to my pride. Father, I regret the choices and decisions I have made because of being prideful.

Holy Spirit, I ask You to come in and convict me. Renew me with steadfast hope, and help me be humble and discerning in all I do, in Jesus' name, Amen!

Spirits to Discern and Cast Out

Ask the Holy Spirit to reveal all the demonic spirits associated with pride that you need to cast out. Out loud, command these spirits to leave: "Spirit of _____, go, in Jesus' name!" You may have to do this several times over a period of time. Do it until you feel peace, a release or a spiritual shift. Spirits often associated with pride:

Arrogance, blocking, criticism, deception, distraction, hardheartedness, haughtiness, hindering, judgment, justification, Leviathan, Lucifer, mind idolatry, Pharisee, pride, rebellion, religious, selfishness, stubborn, unteachable

Prayer of Activation

I call forth and say that I am submissive to God. I release the need for pride and attention. Father God, teach me how to be humble.

Holy Spirit, humble me and convict me in my ways. I declare today that it is not about me, but about exalting the name of Jesus and putting others first. Spirit of the Living God, help me to love as Jesus loved. I receive correction and ask You to come upon me strongly. Create in me a clean heart in which others are more important than myself, and in which I don't need attention, superiority and arrogance manifesting from me. I love You, Holy Spirit. I need You in this—and in every hour, in Jesus' name I pray. Amen!

Declarations to Speak Out

Speak out the following faith declarations and spiritual warfare declarations. Bookmark these pages and come often as necessary to assist you in renewing your mind, transforming your heart and increasing your faith.

Faith Declarations

Make these faith declarations audibly, with power and authority, believing that you will receive them. Speak them out from a position of *I have these*, not *I'm trying to obtain these*. While you transition from pride to humility, read these declarations out regularly to help you grow strong in faith and renew your mind.

- I speak and decree that I have the mind and humility of Christ.
- I speak and declare that I will walk in humility.
- I proclaim that when prideful thoughts come to attack me, I will capture the thoughts and dismiss them quickly, in Jesus' name.
- I capture my thoughts and submit them to the Word of God.
- I speak and call forth that I will be obedient to God and disciplined in all my ways.
- I dissolve any partnership with pride, and any entitlement I have felt to have legal rights to exude pride.
- I have power over the enemy; therefore, I will smash down all prideful thoughts and dismiss them before I entertain them.
- When pride attacks me, I will look to the Lord, glorify His name and read His Word, in Jesus' name!

Spiritual Warfare Declarations

Make these spiritual warfare declarations audibly, with power and authority. When you speak out these declarations, you are taking up your God-given authority to bind and restrict the enemy and counteract future attacks. Declare them repeatedly, until you feel something release in the spiritual atmosphere.

- I command and cast out a spirit of pride, in Jesus' name.
- I eradicate and utterly remove the enemy and his cohorts from their assignment to keep me bound in a spirit of pride.
- I disperse confusion into the enemy's camp and bind and restrict him from operating on his orders to steal, kill and destroy.
- I bind and rebuke, cut off and renounce the spirits of Lucifer, Leviathan and pride from attacking me or attacking my thoughts.
- I order every demonic assignment and hindrance in my life to be aborted of its mission and assignment, in Jesus' name.
- I abolish the powers of darkness hovering around me, trying to cause dissension on my God-given assignment.
- I restrict the plans of the enemy. I speak and decree that I have authority over all things, attacks and assignments.
- I uproot every root that has been placed deep down within my soul, and I break agreement with you, in Jesus' name.
- I instruct the enemy to back off from attacking my mind, my thoughts and my perceptions. You will have no place in me.
- I break off the powers and activation in the spiritual realm of every word curse spoken against me that I am prideful, critical or judgmental, in the name of Jesus!

CHAPTER 7

ANGER

On a scale of 1 to 10, rate each statement below.

1. I can feel anger arise from within me when I get upset.
2. When I am finished reacting in anger, I feel shame, condemnation and regret.
3. I sometimes feel as if I cannot control my anger.
4. I sometimes feel as if I am not being listened to unless I yell and get angry.
5. After I have had an outburst of anger, I question what happened and why I reacted that way.
6. I get frustrated and irritated with other people.
7. I cannot identify the difference between natural anger and holy righteous anger.

When my children were young, I would yell at them when I would get upset. I never hurt them, but I do remember screaming at the top of my lungs on occasion, and going on and on for what seemed like several minutes at a time. I recently was talking to my son about anger, and I asked him if he ever remembered me yelling like that. He told me no. I thank God he does not remember those occasions.

One day when we were camping, I was lying in bed when I heard the Lord say, *I just delivered you from three spirits of anger.*

I physically felt those spirits leave my body. Ever since that day, there is only one time I have ever raised my voice again to the point where I felt as if I could not control it. That is the only time since that I have looked back at the situation and asked myself, *Who is that person?*

Previously, I did not realize when I was manifesting a spirit of anger, but I knew that when I would start to unleash, something nasty would come up. It was uncontrolled anger manifesting through a demonic spirit. I was a born-again Christian at the time, but I did not know until that deliverance experience that a demon could reside in me—in my soul (mind, will and emotions), not in my spirit, where the Holy Spirit resides.

My anger came from a generational curse. I am not glad a demonic spirit was affecting me, but I am thankful to have gone through the experience of deliverance. I am glad now to be able to tangibly notice the difference, and I am glad I have an experience people can compare their own experiences to, so they can self-evaluate whether or not they also have a demon of anger.

The Different Kinds of Anger

Anger is often defined as a strong feeling of being upset or annoyed because of something going wrong or bad. It's a feeling that can make someone want to hurt other people or shout. I believe we have all probably shouted in our lives. The question is, How much have you shouted? And when you start shouting, can you stop, or do you feel out of control?

We have all suffered at one time or another from a person making us angry, or from just being angry ourselves. Anger is a human emotion, an emotion of the soul. What I want to do is show you some of the different kinds of anger we experience, which can include natural anger, anger that causes violence, internal anger, holy righteous anger and self-inflicted or self-induced anger. I also want to help you determine if you are experiencing anger as a natural reaction to a situation, or if you have a demonic spirit manifesting as uncontrolled anger.

Natural anger

Natural anger is raising your voice or spouting off. This anger usually manifests because someone did something that made you mad. It is not anger deeply imbedded within us, but rather anger that happens because of an outside situation. Someone did or said something he or she did not have the right to, and you were unable to control that person's words or actions. The bottom line is that someone else did something to you.

Anger manifested in this manner could be because someone who was disobeying traffic laws pulled out in front of you and almost caused an accident. This is an example of something you were unable to control. Someone else took action carelessly, and you got angry. This kind of anger comes in and you may raise your voice, shout or yell, but then it quickly leaves. I will call it the anger that gets in and gets out. When we have an episode of anger, that is what we want it to do: get in and get out so that it does not manifest into demonic spirits or physical conditions.

Biblical examples of natural anger

In Matthew 18:34, we see an example of something a person did to someone else that caused a reaction: "And his master was angry, and delivered him to the torturers until he should pay all that was due to him." Here the master had given this man grace and had forgiven his debt. The man then went and demanded payment from someone else who owed him. The master heard of it, got angry and had him thrown in prison. The master's reaction was due to something his servant did that he could not control. His anger was a reaction to an unfair action against another man. This is anger influenced by another person.

Miriam and Aaron were angry with Moses out of envy (see Numbers 12). Esau was angry with Jacob because Jacob tricked him out of their father's blessing (see Genesis 27:41–46). Potiphar was angry because he believed Joseph betrayed him (see Genesis 39:11–20). These people got angry because of outward situations. There is a saying, "No one can make you angry. You choose to be angry." Did these people choose to be angry? Could they have minimized their anger or chosen to feel differently?

Miriam and Aaron were angry with Moses out of envy, but isn't envy an inward emotion we should have control over? We should not be envious or jealous. The more we pursue our walk with the Lord and our inner healing, the less we will exhibit fleshly emotions. Instead of being envious of Moses, Miriam and Aaron should have been praising and thanking the Lord for the opportunity and favor given Moses. This is similar to what we experience today. We get envious of what other people have instead of being happy for them. We are selfish, and selfishness is a key root behind anger. Instead of rejoicing with people in what they have, we often use it to remind ourselves of what we don't have. So we find ourselves becoming competitive and jealous.

Esau was angry with Jacob because he was tricked out of his birthright blessing. This was betrayal, and unfortunately, people are going to betray us. Someone Esau loved, someone he was close to, betrayed him. What we have to remember when feelings of anger and betrayal come is to release those emotions as quickly as possible. Betrayal can fester and make us build up self-protective walls so that we no longer trust people and have difficulty allowing new relationships into our lives. Jacob was being selfish and allowed betrayal to come forth. When we identify the correlation between anger and selfishness, it will assist us in dealing with people, extending them grace, and not allowing ourselves to get angry due to their actions or responses.

Potiphar was angry with Joseph because he believed that this servant he trusted, whom he even considered a friend, had betrayed him. Joseph did not betray Potiphar, however. He was loyal. Potiphar could have changed the situation by looking at the facts about Joseph and discerning his loyalty. Instead, Potiphar reacted in anger. We, too, need to step back and take a look at a situation before reacting. When we get angry, we need to do what we teach our children to do—count to ten. Taking a step back before we speak allows the reactionary part of our brain to settle down and the forebrain or thoughtful center to take over. We need to give the Holy Spirit a chance to speak to us about a situation before we respond.

Anger that causes violence

Balaam hit his donkey out of anger: "Balaam's anger was aroused, and he struck the donkey with his staff" (Numbers 22:27). Here Balaam, like many people, hit something out of the anger or rage he was feeling inside.

Spousal or child abuse can occur because a person is angry in this way. Anger builds up and boils, and naturally needs to be released. But in the case of abuse, anger is released on an innocent human being.

A demonic spirit can trigger violent anger. When such a spirit comes in and is not cast out, a lying spirit can also speak to us. Our minds then run rampant with thoughts of hurting other people or ourselves. These are tormenting, lying spirits that come in and speak to a person's mind until he or she cannot resist the temptation to act on the violence.

The ministry of deliverance and casting out of evil spirits such as anger, violence, rage, hate, envy and strife could save a lot of people from hurtful, harmful acts.

Internal anger

Another kind of anger comes from the inside, and Jesus said that what comes out of us from the inside can defile us:

> When He had called all the multitude to Himself, He said to them, "Hear Me, everyone, and understand: There is nothing that enters a man from outside which can defile him; but the things which come out of him, those are the things that defile a man."
>
> Mark 7:14–15

When we manifest anger, it shows us what's inside us. There is a saying, "Hurting people hurt people." When we are hurt by someone else on the inside and have not dealt with that hurt properly, then we manifest that hurt outwardly toward other people. Often, people are not angry with the person they take it out on. They either are angry at a situation in their past or present, or at a situation they are in with you that reminds them of a previous hurt.

One time, a group of people became angry with my husband and me. When the situation was over, we looked back and discovered that one person had suffered a serious family loss, and another was facing severe marital difficulties. In fact, every person we looked at in the situation had suffered a severe hurt in the past that had never been healed. The people involved had stuffed their feelings and had not received the counsel they needed for healing, so they were taking out their past hurts and anger on us. When people take their hurt out on you, don't take it personally. Instead, pray that whatever is consuming them is exposed and that they receive deliverance.

Holy righteous anger

Holy righteous anger is anger that should lead us to take action. Righteous anger consists of getting angry at the things that anger God and then seeking a remedy to correct the wrong being done. This is the kind of anger you experience when you disagree with something that is wrong and you feel led to stand up for your convictions.

Holy righteous anger is all good. It arises from a godly conviction to stand up for yourself and your beliefs. This is a positive emotion.

You do, however, have to watch how you present yourself when you experience this kind of anger. You have to keep the Lord and love first and foremost in your mind and heart. It is a matter of the heart and attitude.

Biblical examples of holy righteous anger

In Mark 3:5, we see an example of righteous anger arising in Jesus: "And when He had looked around at them with anger, being grieved by the hardness of their hearts, He said to the man, 'Stretch out your hand.' And he stretched it out, and his hand was restored as whole as the other."

Jesus was grieved at the hardness of men's hearts, but in the midst of His holy righteous anger, He healed the man. He manifested righteous anger and produced results. Holy righteous anger is anger that leads to action and a positive result, which in this case was healing.

Self-inflicted or self-induced anger

Self-inflicted or self-induced anger is another kind we can experience. We bring this anger on ourselves. Are you a person who does not leave margin in your schedule? We should put extra time in our schedule in case the baby spits up on our outfit when we are getting dressed, or the cat runs out the door and shouldn't be outside, or we spill coffee on our clothes. With margin in our schedule, we have enough time to make the necessary adjustments. Without margin, we can get angry because things aren't going right, and we don't see them as natural happenings and simple mishaps.

Self-inflicted anger happens when we don't leave the house early enough to allow for margin in our schedule. We can experience road rage because we are late and get stuck behind someone who is simply driving the speed limit. We think they should be speeding, just as we are. Now angry, we start yelling at the person in front of us to speed up, move over or get off the road. The person cannot even hear us, so really we are yelling at ourselves.

Anger can also happen when we don't leave room in our commute time for accidents, traffic delays or construction. All of these normal parts of commuting can cause irritation, but we are responsible for some of the anger we induce in ourselves when we don't give ourselves margin in our schedule.

Anger can also happen in our time at home with our family. If we are watching our favorite TV show, the news or a movie and someone starts talking or accidentally walks in front of the TV, how do we respond? We can react in anger at the interruption or distraction. Anger because of these interruptions can indicate irritability or electronic addiction (which I talk more about in chapter 12), now manifested as anger taken out on those we love.

Testing Your Anger Level

We need to test the level of anger we experience and determine if it is natural anger arising out of human emotions or anger coming from a demonic source. When we experience anger, we can become hotheaded and feel the need to spout off and get things off our chest. Anger can manifest when someone has made us mad, or has violated or offended us. Anger can manifest as we allow those wounds to fester. We could also be manifesting severe anger controlled by demonic spirits.

Even though we all will experience times when we get angry, most often we can control those feelings of outrage. The anger we really need to be concerned about is the anger that rises from our belly. When you have a spirit of anger, it will rise up out of the pit of your belly. You start yelling, and you don't stop. You keep yelling and screaming, loudly, and it can go on and on for several minutes. You can actually feel it coming up out of your belly, as though you *have* to release something.

As you grow in your walk with the Lord and pursue your healing, the Holy Spirit will convict you if this is your situation, and you will become aware of the manifestation you are experiencing. You can also self-evaluate when your outburst is finished and ask yourself, *Who was that person? That wasn't me! What just happened? What did I do?*

These thoughts are convictions from the Holy Spirit, along with your natural insights that will come forward and make you more aware that what you are doing is not like you. When you start recognizing the outbursts for what they are, you know you are in the process of deliverance.

Inner healing leads to deliverance. What would happen if people pursued inner healing? Would it be possible not to get angry? You bet! I believe the closer we grow to God, the fewer outbursts we have, and the less the world and what people do and say affect us. As I look over the course of my life, I can see where the anger that once manifested has been replaced by love and peace. Situations that once upset me no longer seem to affect me. I believe the more Kingdom focused we become, the less we let the inadequacies and immaturity of people, or their words and actions, impact us.

Responding to Anger and Irritability

The Bible instructs us about how to answer our own anger: "'Be angry, and do not sin': do not let the sun go down on your wrath" (Ephesians 4:26). Purpose in your heart that you will not give any place to the devil when you get angry. If we get angry, we need to make sure it does not lead us into sin. The anger I mean here is where Satan is trying to provoke us to sin. If we allow the devil to do that, he wins, and the words *devil* and *winning* do not belong together in the same sentence.

Irritability co-labors with anger and triggers it in people. Webster's definition of irritability is "quick excitability to annoyance, impatience, or anger."[1] Irritability consists of reactionary words and body motions such as a dirty look, a disgusted facial expression or swinging an arm quickly through the air. It is that quick snap with a sharp-toned voice. Irritability causes arguments. People who are being irritable often don't realize what they are doing. This behavioral pattern has become a normal reaction in how they behave and speak. Irritability is rude, belittling and inconsiderate, but irritable people often see themselves as simply responding to others, not being irritable.

People who act out in irritability have an unhealed wound from their past that is causing them to react negatively. It is best for us not to react to irritable people, but to ignore their comments or remarks. We are not ignoring the individual; we are ignoring the irritability manifesting through that person. By ignoring someone's sharp response or tone, we are attempting to avoid sin ourselves by not letting that person's irritability cause a negative response in us. If you must respond to an irritable person, say something like "okay" or "I'll pray for you," if appropriate, but don't get into a full-blown conversation with the person. Otherwise, he or she may react defensively, and an outburst of anger could erupt from the demonic spirit within.

Separate the Person and Principality

When you are dealing with a person who manifests anger on a consistent basis, it is helpful to separate the person from the principality. We need to love the person and dislike the principality. "For we do not wrestle against flesh and blood, but against principalities, against powers, against the rulers of the darkness of this age, against spiritual hosts of wickedness in the heavenly places"

1. *Merriam-Webster* online, s.v. "Irritability," https://www.merriam-webster.com/dictionary/irritability.

(Ephesians 6:12). Separate the person you love from the behavior he or she is manifesting. The person you love is still there, but is acting out based on being plagued by a demonic spirit. Don't fault the person and be mean or angry yourself. Seldom do such people realize a demonic spirit is manifesting through them.

When someone you love is yelling at you in a spirit of anger, know when to shut down and shut up. Do not argue with the person. If you do, you are simply arguing with a demonic spirit. When a spirit of anger is manifesting, it has for a brief time taken over the person you know and love, so the person does not hear what you are saying. When you yell back, you are yelling at a demonic spirit that is yelling at you through the person's soul. All this cycle creates is more yelling, more anger, more hurt feelings and more confusion.

Purpose in your mind not to allow such a situation to escalate. Learn to sit down and shut up. Nod your head slightly to acknowledge that you heard the person. Tell him or her that you are not going to have this conversation right now, that you are hanging up the phone or leaving the room and will not participate any further in the conversation until you both can talk in peace and love.

The Faces of Anger

One way anger manifests is that a person looks like his or her normal self on one day, and the next day looks like a completely different person. In the book of Daniel, Nebuchadnezzar's facial expression changed when he was furious: "Then Nebuchadnezzar was full of fury, and the expression on his face changed toward Shadrach, Meshach, and Abed-Nego. He spoke and commanded that they heat the furnace seven times more than it was usually heated" (Daniel 3:19). This was a demon manifesting through his facial expression. His face changed because of the anger and rage within him.

People we talk to and love can do the same thing. When they live angrily, they can look like one person one day and a completely different person the very next day. You can physically see the anger manifesting on their face. When they are manifesting anger like that, leave them alone. You will notice their voice fluctuations; their voice may rise up and get high-pitched, or it may sound angry and deep. If you pay close attention, you can see the person shift from the individual you know and love to the demon that is manifesting through him or her. Be kind, be gentle and be about God's love toward that person.

When in a confrontation with an angry person, don't say anything back. Being silent is the most difficult thing to do sometimes, but what the Father showed me is that when we put our two cents in and argue back, we get hurt. How? If you keep silent, the person can only spew words at you for a moment. But if you argue back, you end up going back and forth. You both say things you don't mean. During the time when ungodly things are being said, you may discover how the person feels inside about something you were previously unaware of. Now you are hurt about something new, and you have added more hurt to what you were already experiencing.

Know that saying something in those situations won't make a difference. We want to control people, and we want to think they will change because we state our opinion. People don't always change as a result of what we say. We want to think they will, but often they don't even listen. It goes in one ear and right out the other. Saying something in anger-filled moments can also cause continual arguments, and more irritation, fighting, yelling and dissension.

Anger Is an Addiction

Anger is addictive. When people get angry, endorphins are released that feed their system. It is an adrenaline rush for them. One in six people become so angry that they feel like hitting another person. These people use anger or the threat of anger to gain control over others. They enjoy having people live in fear of them. They know that if they exude enough anger, their family and friends will react quickly when asked to do something, in fear of the repercussions if they don't comply.

People addicted to anger realize there is power in having others fear getting them angry. They like the power and control that exuding their anger gives them. They also want attention, and exuding anger, even though it is unhealthy, gets them the attention they crave.

Speaking of addictions, not only is anger an addiction in itself; it also causes addictions. Alcohol and drugs are also a tool angry people use, and substance abuse is one of the harmful ways in which it manifests. When people become angry and can't control their circumstances, they may start abusing drugs or alcohol as a way to escape the pain of their situation. Such substance abuse may bring some temporary relief of a naturally occurring problem in their lives, but most of the time the substance abuse also intensifies their anger, compounding the problem further.

Negative Physical Reactions

Anger affects our body in negative ways. When we feel anger arise, we can counteract some of these negative physical responses by breathing in deeply for four seconds, holding it for four seconds, and then exhaling for four seconds.

Our thoughts, feelings, vain imaginations and false scenarios infiltrate our mind when we are angry. Stress, hate and rage infiltrate our body, causing our blood pressure to increase and our muscles to tighten. It also affects our adrenal gland, and it activates our hypothalamus emergency system, affecting a good portion of our body. Anger that affects our health over long periods of time can lead to death. It has been said a lot of heart attacks happen on Super Bowl Sunday because men get so angry and stressed over the football game.

Anger kills in other ways, too, when people use other weapons or objects. A person can use a car, airplane, baseball bat, explosive or firearm. We hear about mass shootings taking place for what seems like no explicit reason. When a shooting takes place, it's due to a demonic spirit of anger, not natural anger.

Various Ways Anger Manifests

Over time, feelings of anger we don't release properly build up. As we experience natural feelings of anger and do not receive healing, it can provide an entry point for a strongman of anger to come in. When our emotions are not balanced over time, they can lead to transitioning from human emotions to manifesting a demonic spirit. Anger can then manifest in a variety of ways.

This explains why a person we never thought could kill someone or never thought would have the emotional determination to pull the trigger on a gun has now committed an unthinkable act. Releasing unhealthy pent-up emotions will assist us in preventing these attacks. So will casting out spirits of anger, rage, violence, and unfairness or a victim mindset.

Anger can manifest in many ways—hurting other people, making impulsive decisions, allowing our emotions to get out of control and the like. Here are some other ways it manifests:

- Terrorist attacks that happen with planes, explosives or guns
- Murder and suicide
- Road rage or even running people down with a car
- Spontaneously quitting a job
- Rebellion and making the wrong decision to hurt someone else emotionally

Holding onto anger is like stockpiling an arsenal full of loaded weapons ready to fire at a moment's notice. The impact can be emotional, when an angry person acts out to hurt someone else's feelings, or it can be physical, when an angry individual does something literally harmful to others.

Casting out anger is imperative in order to protect ourselves, those we love and others. When a demon of anger gets unleashed and released out of someone in a fit of rage, sometimes there is no predicting what that person will do.

A Biblical Rest for Anger

Psalm 4:4 says, "Be angry and do not sin. Meditate within your heart on your bed, and be still. Selah." Rest. Meditate within your heart. As we rest, we go to the place of love with the Father. How can we be angry when we are in that place of love? We are instructed to be still.

We need to be still and not react to things, evaluating each situation to see if there is any merit in being angry. If we go to that place of love with the Father and allow Him to speak to us through a situation, we can release any anger to Him. This goes along with James 1:19, which says, "So then, my beloved brethren, let every man be swift to hear, slow to speak, slow to wrath." If we would truly live by the Word of God, a lot of anger would not even manifest!

The Bible further instructs us in Proverbs 16:32 how to control our anger: "He who is slow to anger is better than the mighty, and he who rules his spirit than he who takes a city." Proverbs 19:11 adds, "The discretion of a man makes him slow to anger, and his glory is to overlook a transgression." We need to be quick to listen and slow to anger. Don't make anger your first reaction. Don't act or react. Pray, discern and be slow to speak.

We need to act in the Spirit and not in the flesh. We get angry because we allow our flesh to respond. We have to have control of our flesh. We need discretion, and using the discernment of the Holy Spirit will assist us in controlling our flesh.

Walking Out Your Deliverance

Anger can lead to many different problems. It brings results that are unproductive and leaves destruction in its wake. Self-evaluate to see if your anger is triggered by a natural reaction to a situation, or if you have a demonic spirit manifesting as uncontrolled anger. Are you someone who likes to be in control, and when you are not, anger manifests? Speak life and peace over situations in which you feel anger arising.

Scriptures on Peace

Proverbs 17:27–28; Romans 14:19; Ephesians 4:29; Philippians 4:7; Colossians 3:15; Hebrews 12:14; 1 Peter 3:10

Prayer of Repentance and Forgiveness

Pray this prayer audibly to repent and release forgiveness:

Heavenly Father, please forgive me for the times I have held onto anger against others. Right now, today, I decide to forgive _____ (insert names). I choose no longer to be angry with them. I release them of their offenses against me. Forgive me for expressing rage, violence, hatred and anger. I forgive myself, and I choose to live in peace. Father, now fill me with Your fruit of the Spirit and help me live a life of emotions that are in line with Your Word, in Jesus' name. Amen!

Spirits to Discern and Cast Out

Ask the Holy Spirit to reveal all the demonic spirits associated with anger that you need to cast out. Out loud, command these spirits to leave: "Spirit of _____, go, in Jesus' name!" You may have to do this several times over a period of time. Do it until you feel peace, a release or a spiritual shift. Spirits often associated with anger:

Accusation, aggressive, anger, argumentative, arrogance, attention, backbiting, bickering, bitterness, boastful, bondage, bullying, complaining, confrontation, crankiness, critical, cruelty, cursing, deception, defensiveness, destroyer, embarrassment, exaggeration, excuses, fighting, generational curse, harassment, hardness of heart, hate, headstrong, hostility, irritability, jealousy, offense, profanity, quarreling, rage, rebellion, selfishness, stubbornness, swearing, temper, tension, violence

Prayer of Activation

Father God, right now in the name of our Jesus, I ask You to impart love, joy, peace, unity, contentment, compromise and forgiveness. Fill me with hope for healing. Help me learn to yield in love, be slow to speak and walk in the Spirit.

Holy Spirit, convict me as I go forth of any unhealthy emotions and any reactions that are not of You. Help me be a better person and live my life in a way that would glorify Your name and exude peace, in Jesus' name. Amen!

Declarations to Speak Out

Speak out the following faith declarations and spiritual warfare declarations. Bookmark these pages and come back to them as often as necessary to assist you in renewing your mind, transforming your heart and increasing your faith.

Faith Declarations

Make these faith declarations audibly, with power and authority, believing that you will receive them. Speak them out from a position of *I have these*, not *I'm trying to obtain these*. While you transition from anger to peace, read these declarations out regularly to help you grow strong in faith and renew your mind.

- I call forth and claim that I will be slow to speak. I will open my ears and be attentive and sensitive to what others are saying.

- I purpose in my heart to be conscious to walk in the Spirit. I will bind my flesh and unnecessary reactions. I will yield when the Spirit is speaking and listen to His instructions on how to handle a situation before I act out.

- I set my mouth apart to be used by the Lord. Father God, consecrate my lips, that only holy words come forth. I decree and declare that my mouth is to be used by God to speak peace and not by the enemy to perpetuate anger.

- I call forth the fruit of the Spirit to manifest in my life. I speak and pronounce that love, joy, peace, longsuffering, kindness, goodness, faithfulness, gentleness and self-control manifest in my life.

- I stand in the strength of the Lord, and as I go about my day, I look to Him to guide me in all my words and give me His wisdom.

- I decree that I am a prayerful person. In moments when I want to react or act, I will not release outbursts of anger. I will pray for the Holy Spirit to lead me in the proper words to release, in Jesus' name.

Spiritual Warfare Declarations

Make these spiritual warfare declarations audibly, with power and authority. When you speak out these declarations, you are taking up your God-given authority to bind and restrict the enemy and counteract future attacks. Declare them repeatedly, until you feel something release in the spiritual atmosphere.

- I refuse to allow the enemy to use my past sins to determine my future. I will not act on the words he wants me to release in anger. I will not allow demonic attacks to infiltrate my life.

- I renounce every angry spirit I have sent forth. I break agreement with the spirits of anger, rage and violence. I deploy angels to activate on assignment and abolish the evil plans of the enemy sent against me.

- I paralyze the powers of darkness attempting to instill in me thoughts of hate, suicide, anger and destruction. Every vain imagination and false scenario, I annihilate you with the fire of God. Be removed of your assignment, in Jesus' name.

- I uproot and send away the plans of the spoiler against myself, my family and ministry. I speak and decree that I am like a tree with my roots firmly placed in the ground. I stand on the foundation of Jesus Christ, and I release the peace of God.

- I speak and decree that I have the *shalom* peace of God. I thank You, Father, that You are peace and that Your peace resides in me. Since I am made in Your image, therefore peace must be released from me because peace is in You.

- I call off every demonic assignment against me and against my thinking. I rebuke and take authority over spirits of unfairness, judgment and critical spirits. I will not partner with these demonic entities to wreak havoc in my life. My life is prosperous, and God's Word will prosper in my life, in Jesus' name.

CHAPTER 8

REJECTION

Self-Assessment-Spirit of Rejection

On a scale of 1 to 10, rate each statement below.

1. I assume my friends are upset with me when they don't reach out and call me or return my calls.

2. I ask others how they are doing, but I seldom talk about my own feelings.

3. I assume people are talking about me when I walk into a room and all of a sudden they are quiet.

4. I feel left out if I am not included in a lunch date, invited to be part of a ministry team or included in a meeting.

5. I try to be a peacemaker and do things to make another person's life easier.

6. I tell people to leave me alone, when really I want someone to ask me what's wrong.

7. Physical touch is very important to me, and I feel a great need to receive and give hugs.

Rejection comes in different ways, but we have all suffered some level of rejection. It is what we do with that rejection that matters, and how we handle it in our lives. When I look over the course of my life, I realize I have been fortunate to suffer only little pinches of rejection. I have been surrounded by people with a strongman of rejection, however, so I have learned a lot in the process of seeing these people seek their deliverance.

Until people go through a healing process, rejection can repeat its detrimental cycle and become a malady in their lives. People who are rejected are often people pleasers who constantly work to find acceptance, yet they don't feel accepted. The truth is that only Jesus Christ can bring us the acceptance we seek.

Rejected people feel inadequate. Self-condemnation and insecurity plague them consistently. They are plagued by continual thoughts of *What did I do wrong? And why don't people like me?* They feel that nothing they do is ever good enough.

A spirit of rejection enters someone for a variety of reasons. Finding the root cause—going deep into your inner wounds and feelings—is key to finding freedom. Discovering rejection's entry point and where seeds of rejection were planted will assist you. Determining the cause will allow you to use your power and authority in Christ strategically to dislodge the spirit of rejection operating through your emotions.

The healing process of walking through rejection and releasing forgiveness toward the people who have hurt you is instrumental in receiving freedom. Knowing who you are in Christ and what the Word of God says about you is equally important in understanding your true identity and finding deliverance.

Ways Rejection Enters

Rejection begins in the womb for babies who were unplanned, unwelcomed pregnancies. My husband was an unplanned pregnancy.

His mother got pregnant at forty years of age. Several times, she spoke out her disappointment with the pregnancy. Words are powerful. Words spoken aloud about not wanting a child, or other negative words about a pregnancy and the coming baby, allow the spiritual realm to activate on those words.

Even if rejection does not start in the womb, it usually enters people before they reach adulthood. In your childhood years, you have not yet become equipped in how to rebuke rejection. That makes your school years and adolescence huge entry points for rejection, and it therefore becomes part of you. The majority of people I have ministered to either suffered family rejection or school rejection that ended up following them for years and creating a pattern of rejection in their lives.

Look back at your school years, even as early as elementary school. Did you ever feel left out and unimportant, perhaps if you were the last person picked for a team or to partner on a project? What thoughts or feelings arose in you? When you think today of the people who rejected you or did not pick you for things, do you still have ill feelings toward them? Was there a person or a teacher that picked on you? What about your friends? Were you in a group of friends, or were you unaccepted and not someone other kids wanted to be friends with? Were you made fun of as a child for your weight, appearance or actions? Were you bullied? Did you want to hang around popular people, cheerleaders or the jocks, only to discover that they would not accept you?

If reading this and thinking about these instances or people brings forth feelings of resentment or negative emotions, then you need healing from a spirit of rejection. The true test of healing is that we can talk about a negative experience without manifesting a negative emotion. If any of these questions lit a spark in you, take a moment now to go through the process of forgiveness (revisit chapter 2 for help with that, if needed). Make sure you have released every offender you can identify of the offense he or she committed against you.

Your mind and heart may have received rejection so many times that you don't even realize you are living in it. Unfortunately, you accept this state of feeling rejected as part of your personality and your character traits, and you think nothing is wrong. The way your mind has been thinking seems normal to you, even though it is unhealthy and unproductive. You accept the negative thoughts that plague you, because you don't know the difference. It is not until later in life, when people are seeking their healing—as you are doing now—that they explore the possibility that the feelings of rejection they have experienced for so long are not normal feelings.

Lying Spirits

Behind every spirit of rejection is a lying spirit that attacks your mind, activating vain imaginations and other accusing spirits. It is the lies we believe that trigger rejection. In fact, lying spirits trigger a lot of things: negativity, pessimism, insecurity and un-worthiness. Your thoughts become a tangled mess of assuming the worst, and you don't see the reality of a situation. You think negatively of yourself, and you believe everyone is out to get you and no one likes you.

The challenge is in recognizing the lying spirits. You see your thoughts as the truth, when really it is the enemy plaguing your mind. Some of our minds even run wild with false scenarios and vain imaginations. We have all heard thoughts in our head such as *you're no good* or *you're never going to amount to anything*. We will entertain these thoughts until the lies are exposed and the enemy's tactics are revealed.

We need to keep our mind focused on Christ so it does not run rampant. Lies that we believe cause emotional triggers and roots of rejection to become deeply planted within our soul. As I said before, some of these thoughts may seem normal to you, but now that you have been educated about this, take some time to determine the source of such thoughts.

Jobs and Relationships

Jobs and relationships can also be entry points for a spirit of rejection. Questions rage through your mind when you apply for a job and don't get it. You go in with the right qualifications and the desire in your heart, and then they pass you up for someone else. You don't understand because you did everything right, but it all ended up wrong. That kind of rejection attacks the seat of your emotions. People have committed suicide over being rejected for a job.

Dating people and getting married is a normal part of life for most of us, but then a relationship goes sour and the other person rejects us, and we don't understand what we did wrong. We may end up sitting around thinking about how, if only we could have played out scenarios differently, the outcome might have been different. Rejection sets in, and we give up hoping for that special someone to love.

I have counseled numerous strong Christian women who have great careers and have their finances in order. These beautiful ladies are committed to the Lord, yet in their thirties and forties they are still single and are unable to find "Mr. Right." They continually feel rejected in relationships that don't work out, or by all the men who see them and never ask them out. The rejection they experience then drives these women even harder to find Mr. Right so they can feel accepted. What they need to know is that Mr. Right is found in a personal relationship with Jesus. Looking to Him first and foremost as their Bridegroom, and trusting God the Father to send along their human mate in His timing, is where they will find hope and healing.

Ministry

Rejection in the ministry can permeate your life in several ways. There is prayer time rejection, when people want someone other than you to pray for them. There is feeling rejected by a pastor or leader when you thought you had a really great idea and leadership did not jump onboard. There are what I call rejecting actions against itinerant ministers, when you are traveling for the Lord, and those you minister to either don't receive you or feel in competition with what you bring. I will cover each of these topics in a little more detail to bring forth an exposure of rejection, and then to bring forth healing.

Prayer Time Rejection

Imagine that you are ministering during prayer time at a service or event, and you see a person approaching the front of the prayer line and then allowing other people to go on ahead. Clearly, that person prefers to wait for prayer from the "more anointed" pastor or conference speaker next to you, rather than having you pray for him or her.

Depending on where you are in your walk with the Lord and whether or not you are in a relationship with the person who sidestepped you, you could take in rejection from that situation. You could feel as if your prayers are not good enough. Let me tell you, your prayers are good enough! When you open your mouth and speak out, God listens!

Feeling Rejected by Pastors or Leaders

Unfortunately, members of the Body of Christ have suffered emotional attacks within the Church itself. Our churches would be a better place if more of us received the deliverance we so desperately need. Many people have experienced betrayals, offense and hurt from those within their own Christian community.

Suppose you want to deposit into the Kingdom of God, and you have some great ideas about what your place of ministry could do even better. When you approach the pastor or leaders, however, they deny your requests, sometimes without even prayerfully considering them.

Now you feel rejected, and you feel you are not valued in the Body of Christ, which in turn leads to feeling offended at the leadership. Maybe you even applied for a volunteer or paid position in the ministry and they did not choose you, so you also feel rejected that they chose someone else over you.

The offense and rejection we pick up in the Church can get so bad that church splits occur. Or people keep hopping from one church to the next just to find a place where they will feel accepted, loved and valued.

Rejection of Itinerate Ministry

Itinerate ministers, evangelists, prophets and (I will add) deliverance ministers often experience rejecting actions against them. I call these things "rejecting actions" rather than rejection itself, because I hope leaders have worked through their rejection issues to the point where they can dismiss such attacks without letting these actions become an entry point for a spirit of rejection. I know this is not always the case, so I encourage you to get this book into the hands of any itinerant ministers you know who need to work through the healing process from this kind of rejection.

Traveling ministers often end up in competition with the local pastor. It is not purposeful competition, but someone who comes in operating in a strong anointing can intimidate someone who is still growing in his or her knowledge of the Lord. Competition, jealousy and self-exaltation can appear in the host ministry in such cases. When host leadership sees you come in as a traveling minister and flowing in a strong anointing, they could decide to prevent it from happening again—so as not to take their people's focus off themselves. The host church then tells you, "Thank you for coming. We had an awesome service!" And the pastor goes on to say, "We must have you back again!" But the call never comes.

You reach out to follow up and schedule another meeting, but the leadership ignores your messages and calls. Or they make up excuses about why they can't have you back. It all leaves you fighting off a spirit of rejection and wondering what you said or did wrong when you ministered at their church or spent time with them in private. If the word you preached offended them, they probably needed the conviction. You ponder your actions, however, because you want to search your soul and make sure you did everything you could to honor the Lord.

The truth of the matter is that you probably did nothing wrong. That pastor or those leaders decided not to have you back because of their own insecurity, intimidation, fear, jealousy, competition or whatever they were struggling with at the time. Don't take in the wondering thoughts and the lying spirits as rejection. As long as you were obedient, preached the Word and ministered as Jesus would, that's what matters.

Family Roots of Rejection

Rejection attacks us within our immediate families, and we need to conquer it so it does not cause disunity and strife. For example, rejection can come forth in sibling rivalry. Growing up, you may clearly witness favoritism in your family relationships. Or when a family has a child with special needs or behavioral or medical issues that require extra attention, feelings of being ignored, invisible or unimportant can happen to the other children. The children who are well may receive less attention, thereby causing the onset of feelings of rejection due to the special needs of their sibling.

Divorce is another reason that children experience rejection. When one parent leaves home, children will often feel abandoned and rejected by that parent. Rejection can also continue in a family's generational line through a grandparent, aunt, uncle or other relative who is unloving, abusive or disengaged toward a child.

Search your hearts by stepping back and looking at your childhood. Try to discern where some of these things could have happened to you. If they did, I want to work with you to root out all the possible seeds of rejection that could be infiltrating your soul and manifesting in your life today in seen and unseen ways.

Let's also evaluate other areas in a family where rejection can take root. Parents can feel rejected by their children. If you are a parent, do your children take you for granted, ignore you or choose not to implement your suggestions? When you are investing in your children and trying to parent them the best way you know how, it can feel like rejection if they don't implement your ideas, or if they seem unappreciative of you and don't desire to spend time with you. Your hurt feelings can cause a repetitive cycle of rejection through these acts on the part of your children.

Rejection can enter through a marriage relationship. If you are married, does your spouse know your love language and respond to your needs? Does he or she consider your feelings, or selfishly want his or her needs satisfied? Is your spouse spending time with you, or spending free time going out with other friends or staying at work longer hours than seem necessary? Does your spouse allow you to speak out your opinion and make suggestions freely, or does he or she get irritated with your input and snap back at you? These actions can add up to rejection and even lead to divorce.

Identifying these inadequacies in your marriage relationship can assist you in creating a prayer list for your spouse. You can pray and ask the Holy Spirit to convict and change your spouse, and to root out any strongholds he or she may have. As you take these issues to prayer before your Father, hopefully it will bring about change, which will enhance your marriage and remove the emotions of rejection you are experiencing.

Asking the Hard Questions

Self-evaluation and examination can assist in exposing and revealing rejection at its roots. We don't often see the pockets of rejection in our lives if we don't take the time to look for them.

A spirit of pride can also co-labor with rejection to prevent us from seeing the rejection we truly suffer from. Asking ourselves some hard questions and then reflecting on the answers could lead us to discover areas of our life where we need to root out rejection.

For example, ask yourself, *Do I have difficulty receiving correction? Do I resent authority?* People who can't receive correction and always feel the need to input their own thoughts and ideas struggle with fear of failure. They are also afraid of being wrong, because if they are wrong, they feel rejected. In their mind, they cannot comprehend that they simply might be wrong, because it makes them feel they have screwed up again.

Other hard questions to ask yourself might be these: *Do I have to feel or appear superior? Am I adamant about my opinions? Do I enjoy being in control?* If you experience any of these feelings, spend some time seeking out what triggers your emotions of rejection, or what incidents in your past triggered them. When you can correlate the triggers with the emotions, you can discover the root causes of rejection and cast them out.

Craving Acceptance

Rejected people have an unnatural need for people to accept them. They constantly put themselves out there to do things people will applaud. They will sacrifice their time and their own needs to make things easier on another person, even though it makes things harder for themselves. Words of affirmation are their form of acceptance. It becomes their love language, along with quality time, because remember, they require attention. Pleasing other people and getting a constant pat on the back for a job well done is their means of finding acceptance. This unnatural need for getting people to accept them can become codependency and lead to an unhealthy relationship heading for demise.

People pleasers will wait on their spouse hand and foot. I have seen this go to the extreme. For example, a woman living in fear of upsetting her man and being rejected will go out and buy his tobacco, cigarettes or alcohol even when he could have stopped to get his own supply on his way home from work. She will purchase alcohol for him even when she knows he drinks excessively and she wants him to stop. Extreme people-pleasers like this will do everything for their spouse, so their spouse does not have to lift a finger. It is great to be loving and kind, but we don't want to serve people to the point where they don't do anything for themselves. We have to be careful not to enable their actions.

People pleasers don't want conflict and live in fear of it. They will do anything to make anyone happy. In order to be released from people-pleasing, you have to start saying no to doing everything for your friends and family. You have to allow them to do some things on their own, which will equip them to become self-sufficient and not depend on you all the time. It will also help you move toward freedom.

One woman took action and started making her husband clean up his own reading material, which he was always leaving piled up by the couch until she picked it all up. Finally one day, she tossed him a bag and said, "Pick up your own mess."

Your family and friends won't appreciate it when you stop doing things for them. You will experience some resistance, but you must draw back from doing what you never should have been doing for them in the first place.

A Hierarchy of Spirits

In the demonic realm, there is a hierarchy of spirits. There are strongman spirits such as a spirit of deception or a seducing spirit; these strongmen are above other spirits. There are also spirits like a spirit of fear that are driving forces behind other spirits attacking our mind. Let's look at some of these and how they work.

A spirit of deception

Above the lying spirits we hear attacking us in our mind is a strongman spirit of deception that deceives us into believing a lie. The lies this spirit can put forth attack us so much that we start to believe them. When we take in a lie for so long, we have co-labored with it, and the lie becomes a strongman.

Rejection is always manifesting with lying and deceptive spirits, along with several other spirits listed at the end of the chapter. Until people realize that rejection co-labors with other spirits, the rejection is not successfully cast out of their lives. All the co-laboring spirits also have to be cast out.

A seducing spirit

A strongman above the rejection spirit is a seducing spirit. I am not describing a sexual, lustful spirit; this seducing spirit lures you into wrong thinking. In the natural, a sexual spirit draws you into being sexually attracted to someone inappropriately. You think about the person even when you are not with him or her. Correlate the natural draw of sexual spirits with the spiritual lure of a seducing spirit. When you feel rejected, your thoughts are focused on the rejection and what you experienced. When you know you have a problem with an unhealthy desire or lust toward pornography and masturbation, you try to refocus your eyes and thoughts and not act out in perversion. It is the same when you realize that there is a luring, seducing spirit in operation above your feelings of rejection. You try to overcome the thoughts and focus your mind in another direction, but you can't because the draw is so strong that you can't pull yourself out of wrong thinking.

In times like these, when you can't get ahold of your mind, you are being afflicted with a demonic spirit. You are undergoing a spiritual attack that is infiltrating your mind and luring you to focus on the lying and deceptive spirits. The spirits are seducing you, luring you to keep your mind focused on your defeat. You hear thoughts that tell you, *Look, that person rejected you. Look, they did it again.* Seducing spirits keep you on that hamster wheel going round and round, thinking about the same old cycle of rejection. The seducing spirit has to be cast out by name.

A spirit of fear

Behind rejection is a *spirit of fear*. Fear pulls you into rejection. When you have experienced rejection, you fear the thing that caused those feelings. You are afraid of being rejected again, so you usually don't trust God about the thing you fear.

This may involve a fear of friendships, for example. If you are feeling insecure in a relationship, you fear losing that relationship. You do not believe for God to provide you with good friends. You have a lack of trust, which leads to fear and manifests as rejection.

Or this may involve a fear of financial provision. If you experience rejection in a job, you could then have a fear of failure. Fear of financial provision is usually tied to insecurity. When you experience rejection at work, depending on the reason, it could make you afraid of losing your job. In your fear, you then stop trusting God to be your financial provider.

Rejection you experience in different areas of your life can lead to a fear of whatever lies behind that rejection. You need to go deep and recognize what is triggering rejection, and identify it. If you can relate to having a spirit of rejection, also ask yourself, *Have I struggled with spirits of fear?* You may not think you are a fearful person and may not see how the two spirits operate together, but they always do. Why does rejection paralyze and grip you? It is because of fear.

Now take a moment to work through your inner healing and deliverance by asking yourself, *What things do I fear?* Each answer you come up with will be one of your root causes that we want to discover. Write those things down so you can more easily identify and deal with whatever it is that you fear. When you discover what you fear, renounce it, break agreement with it and dislodge it.

Familiar Spirits

Familiar spirits are just that—spirits that are familiar with us. They have observed how we think and react, and they know how to jerk our chain to cause an unproductive response. Familiar spirits operate alongside seducing spirits and know how to bind our mind.

Demons are familiar with you because of what you speak out into the spiritual atmosphere. You speak out things such as, "I feel rejected," or "This person did this to me." But the words we use to speak out our feelings can be detrimental to us in the spiritual realm. So if you don't have something positive to say, don't say it.

Familiar spirits cause the same problems to keep repeating in your life. What cycles, seasons and patterns seem to repeat themselves? For example, do your friendships seem to revolve around a certain pattern? Do they seem to accelerate and then take a nose dive downward? Do you have people becoming your best friend and then a few years later leaving you, only to have a new friend come into the picture and also leave? Or does it seem as if you have had a lot of friendships where control was an issue, which ended in loss and destruction for you? This is a familiar spirit at work to cause distraction, dissension and destruction in your life.

People who live in continual financial insufficiency are often under attack by a familiar spirit. No matter how hard they try, they get hammered over and over again with financial setbacks and losses. At times, we make unwise choices with our money, but if ridiculous financial mishaps occur on a frequent, repetitive basis, a familiar spirit could be in operation.

Fear of Rejection

Fear of rejection paralyzes us and stunts our spiritual gifts. How many times have you had discernment about something, or a word of knowledge, or an unction to pray for healing over a person, or a prophetic word to release, but you have not followed through? Sometimes we don't approach our ministry leaders or others to release what God has given us because the fear of rejection rises in us that the person we approach will not allow us to release what we have. Or we fear that the person is not going to receive what we have to say or pray. Lying spirits infiltrate our thoughts, having us think, *Who am I to share that word? What if they say no?* We hold back in fear of being rejected, which affects our prophetic destiny and ministry calling.

We can usually identify major rejection in our life, but we don't see all the little pinches along the way that still hold us back from the fullness of God. My husband once used the analogy of BBs and a shotgun shell. He said that to get hit with one BB or even two does not hurt, but when you take all those BBs and fill an empty shotgun shell and seal it up, that shotgun shell can kill. Rejection unidentified is like all those BBs. By themselves, their little sting does not seem to matter, but over the years, as they build up inside and fill us up, they are like that shotgun shell that kills.

Fleeting thoughts of painful circumstances and happenings plague our minds daily. When we don't identify them for what they are as rejection, we are in denial. How can you be healed and delivered of something that you don't acknowledge you have and that you are in denial over? Exposing the enemy and the elements of our soul that need healing is crucial to receiving our full deliverance. We should not only want deliverance from the big things that are plaguing us; we should also desire deliverance from every area of our life where we are afflicted.

When rejection attempts to set in, remember that God accepts you. Your focus needs to shift from worrying about what people think to thinking about how God accepts you. Taking in feelings of rejection is a choice. Instead of taking in people's rejection of you, take in, believe and live in the acceptance of God. Have this attitude and mentality: *No one can reject me, because God accepts me!* Renew your mind and walk out your freedom.

Rejection Commands and Demands

Rejection is self-centered and causes us to demand people's time and attention without even realizing it. Then we feel rejected because they cannot satisfy the unspoken demand we are putting on them. Rejected people don't speak out their own need. Instead, they stand around waiting for someone to notice, or for someone to ask them a question or poke and pry into their emotions to get them to release. Rejected people don't want to tell you what is wrong, because they are people pleasers who want to make sure they are making you happy. They will hold back and wait for you to approach them, even though they are desperate to release their feelings.

If you are living in rejection, you don't talk about yourself unless someone leads you to it. You stand around waiting for someone to ask how you are today. Meanwhile, you feel as if you are dying inside. Your face looks like a lost puppy dog, and inside you are thinking, *I'm here! Do you notice me? I don't want to ask you anything, but I really want you to ask me how I am.*

You have a voice. Use it. When you don't release your voice, you are adopting a victim mentality and the devil is keeping you in bondage. Your freedom releases as you begin to talk and speak your mind, and as you believe that what you have to say and what you feel matters. We need to walk out our deliverance by taking physical actions. To find freedom, one action rejected people need to take is to speak out. They need to learn to cast down the fear that prevents them from talking.

I do want to caution you that as you begin to speak out, you may have some abrupt outbursts where you say things differently than the way you had intended. When you have not voiced your opinion in so long and you start to speak out, occasionally it will come out wrong. Correct yourself with the person you are speaking to and ask forgiveness for any wrong word choices or sharp tones.

Rejection's Accomplices

Along with rejection come some accomplices that co-labor along-side it. Isolation is one of rejection's accomplices that provides a false sense of security. Jealousy is another of its accomplices, serving as a mask for rejection itself.

People with rejection will isolate themselves. What do you do when someone upsets you? Your first reaction is probably either to shut up or to spout off. Afterward, you usually withdraw to refocus. Ask yourself why you feel the need to withdraw and have some quiet time when you get upset. Is it because you want to isolate yourself so you can wallow in self-pity, or is it because you want to take it to the Lord in prayer and find *shalom*?

Jealousy may also arise, often as a mask for rejection. How does jealousy reveal itself? A friend of yours may take another friend out for lunch. Suppose you witness them at a restaurant together. You begin to feel bad and wonder why one asked the other to lunch instead of asking you. The jealousy you feel is really a spirit of rejection. The rejection you experience makes you feel left out and hurt. Jealousy is a backdoor way to recognize rejection.

Giving for the Right Reason

When it comes to gift giving, are you giving for the right reason? Sometimes people subconsciously give gifts out of a fear of rejection. People pleasers love to make other people feel good, and in giving a gift, they find the acceptance they crave.

It is not so different from when a man buys his wife flowers after a fight. He is saying, "I'm sorry," but also saying, "I want you to accept me."

If you are a gift giver, self-evaluate and ask the Holy Spirit to expose your reasons for giving. Whenever you give a gift, pray about it. Ask the Spirit, *Am I supposed to buy this person a gift? What do You want me to purchase?*

Then test the discernment you received in prayer a second time to make sure you are confident that the Spirit of the Lord was speaking to you, and that it was not your own thoughts you misidentified as discernment. Do this by asking yourself, *Would I have peace if I bought this gift? Am I purchasing it because I want to and because the Holy Spirit laid it on my heart, or because I have an ulterior motive?*

You Have Value

What thoughts plague your mind that you have difficulty rebuking? Get rid of the mind-plaguing thoughts and stir your gift. You have something to offer the world. You have a gift inside you.

When you get ahold of your mind, you will walk in victory. When a thought comes in, say, "This is a lie, and I am not choosing to believe this lie." Speak it out, right there! Penetrate the spiritual realm with your declaration, saying out loud, "Devil, I forbid you to speak that lie to my mind!" Then move on and dismiss the thought.

Until we can get control of our minds, how can we be effective? The battle is not always with a demon; it is also with gaining control of our own thoughts. The mind is a battlefield.

The Lord has used me personally to deliver many of my friends and team members from a spirit of rejection. It appears to me that in the process of healing rejection, the Lord will often bring a good friend into someone's life who will love that person unconditionally. Don't reject that friendship if this is the case with you. Accept what the friendship has to offer. Don't push the person away, which is a normal reaction so you don't get hurt again. The person is there to help you in your healing and truly be your friend.

A friend God sends into your life in these circumstances also has a lot of value. Here are some characteristics such a friend will have who is sent by God to assist you in being delivered from rejection:

- Your friend will understand that your friendship won't be perfect. He or she will love you through your healing process and forgive you when you make mistakes in the relationship.
- Your friend will be patient, loving, forgiving and compassionate.
- Your friend will hold you accountable for pursuing your healing process.
- You can trust the advice your friend will offer during the process. This person is usually sent by God and is hearing from the Lord.
- Your friend will understand that miscommunication can happen in texting and emailing. Clearly express your feelings and state your intentions.
- Don't assume that something your friend says is negative. If something he or she said upsets you, be aware that a lying spirit is attacking you. Expose the enemy and the lying spirit by asking your friend to clarify what he or she meant.
- Your friend will give you the space you need and won't overburden you by constantly reaching out to you to check on you. Don't assume you did anything wrong if he or she is distant. The friend will be seeking the Holy Spirit for wisdom on when to contact you and when to give you space.

Walking Out Your Deliverance

The most important thing in finding healing from rejection is taking each thought captive. Recognize the negative thoughts as lying spirits attacking you, and command them to go, in Jesus' name. Renew your mind by knowing that God is the only Person who can fulfill all your needs. Look to Him, the Author and Finisher of life. Know that people will disappoint you, but He will never fail you. When you know God loves and accepts you (and truly, that's all that matters), people can never make you feel rejected.

Scriptures on Acceptance

Psalm 56:11; Jeremiah 1:5; 29:11; John 6:37; Romans 8:28, 31; 15:13; Hebrews 13:6

Prayer of Repentance and Forgiveness

Pray this prayer audibly to repent and release forgiveness:

Heavenly Father, I forgive _____ (insert names), people who I feel have rejected me. I forgive my mom and dad, my siblings and other family members for moments of rejection. I choose today to forgive everyone in my life, including classmates, co-workers, friends and acquaintances, for my perception or the reality of them rejecting me. Help me have a clean heart and go forward in Your love and power. I repent of being a people pleaser and taking in emotions of rejection. Help me see myself as a victor, not a victim. Help me rise up and use my voice, and be a blessing to the Kingdom of God, in Jesus' name. Amen!

Spirits to Discern and Cast Out

Ask the Holy Spirit to reveal all the demonic spirits associated with rejection that you need to cast out. Out loud, command these spirits to leave: "Spirit of _____, go, in Jesus' name!" You may have to do this several times over a period of time. Do it until you feel peace, a release or a spiritual shift. Spirits often associated with rejection:

Attention, control, deception, familiar spirits, fear, fear of failure, fear of rejection, hurt, insecurity, lying, people pleasing, rejection, seducing, self-rejection, vain imaginations

Prayer of Activation

I receive the impartation of the love and acceptance of God into my mind, heart and every area of my life. I stand in faith, accepted by God, relying on and leaning on Him for my every love and support.

Holy Spirit, come fill me now to Your fullness. I receive Your acceptance and bind my mind to the mind of Christ, and I hold every thought captive to the Word of God, in Jesus' name. Amen!

Declarations to Speak Out

Speak out the following faith declarations and spiritual warfare declarations. Bookmark these pages and come back to them as often as necessary to assist you in renewing your mind, transforming your heart and increasing your faith.

Faith Declarations

Make these faith declarations audibly, with power and authority, believing that you will receive them. Speak them out from a position of *I have these*, not *I'm trying to obtain these*. While you transition from rejection to acceptance, read these declarations out regularly to help you grow strong in faith and renew your mind.

- I will capture every thought and will not accept the lies trying to penetrate my mind.
- I speak and decree that God accepts me. He has chosen me and loves me.
- I proclaim that my relationships are strong and healthy. I extend forgiveness and grace to those in need.

- I have control over my feelings; I do not allow my feelings to control me.
- I am a new creation in Christ. Old patterns of thinking and old ways of behaving are gone.
- I renew my mind and choose not to believe that others are talking about me or leaving me out, which in return makes me feel rejected.
- I will study the Word of God to learn my identity in Christ and renew my mind, in Jesus' name.

Spiritual Warfare Declarations

Make these spiritual warfare declarations audibly, with power and authority. When you speak out these declarations, you are taking up your God-given authority to bind and restrict the enemy and counteract future attacks. Declare them repeatedly, until you feel something release in the spiritual atmosphere.

- I speak to every distraction in my life, and I command it to be gone, in Jesus' name.
- Strongman of rejection that has followed me through my life, I command you to cease and desist in your attacks against me, in Jesus' name.
- I rebuke and renounce participation with every lying spirit. I will not believe your lies. I will stand strongly on the Word of God as my truth.
- I deploy angelic activity to be released and be activated on assignment to release my destiny.
- I speak and decree that I will no longer be a people pleaser. I do not have to do certain things to get people to love me. I am loved by God.
- I announce to the demonic realm that I am dangerous in my prayer life and that I am going to rise up and fight every stronghold in my life.

- I declare that Jesus died on the cross to take the rejection that plagued me. I receive the accomplished work of the cross and leave rejection on the cross.
- Rejection and every negative thought that leads to rejection, I dismiss you. My mind is filled with every good and perfect thing, in Jesus' name.

CHAPTER 9

UNWORTHINESS AND PASSIVITY

Self-Assessment Test—Spirits of Unworthiness and Passivity

On a scale of 1 to 10, rate each statement below.

1. I don't always feel worthy to be used by God.
2. I am unsure if God can forgive all my sins.
3. I can't look in the mirror unclothed and say, "I love myself; I love what I see."
4. I am a better giver than receiver.
5. I can't forgive myself for some things in my past. Saying "I forgive myself" is hard.
6. I feel shame, condemnation and regret because of my past.
7. I define my inward self by my outward appearance.

I remember my husband coming home years ago from a spiritual retreat and telling me he was being called into ministry. I stayed on the couch for three days and cried. I did not feel good enough to be a pastor's wife. I knew there were sins I had committed, and I did not know how God could use me, a sinner, in ministry. Years later, I had some more slight bouts with unworthiness. (I say *slight* because when you are moving forward into victory, your battle with something gets easier each time.) I knew God was calling me to make a great impact for His Kingdom, and I questioned, *Who am I? I'm just a normal person. Why me?*

Why you? Why me? Because Christ is in us, the hope of glory (see Colossians 1:27). We are worthy because He is worthy, and He lives in us. Period. End of story. There should be no arguments past the statement that we are worthy because He is worthy and lives in us.

Unworthiness is an emotion that prevents us from moving ahead in life successfully, into our God-given destiny. God needs us to move past these feelings so He can use us at our full potential. Unworthiness is attached to how we feel about ourselves. When we feel unworthy, we feel shame and a lack of love toward ourselves. We think about our past failures and how we must have disappointed God or other people, and these thoughts lead to feelings of unworthiness.

Left undealt with, emotions such as unworthiness can lead to a spiritual stronghold. When we have any unhealthy emotion from which we do not receive inner healing, over time that emotion builds up within us and opens such a door. Thus, an emotion undealt with leads to a demonic entry point and a demonic spirit.

When we have sinned and have not forgiven ourselves and received Christ's forgiveness, we feel bad. We regret our past mistakes, whatever they were. Sins like committing adultery, stealing, lying, being angry, drinking too much, abusing our kids, having premarital sex, being caught in a cycle of pornography, and many others keep us living in a constant state of guilt and remorse. The guilt and remorse make us believe that God cannot use us, either in the present or the future.

This is a lie of the enemy! The enemy wants us to believe that we are unclean and sinful and can never be used by God. If we buy into that lie, the devil succeeds in both paralyzing us in the moment and detouring our destiny. In our mind and heart, we start thinking that we will never be good enough to move forward with the plans God has for us. Then these thoughts that we will never be good enough allow us to become passive.

Passivity Detours Our Destiny

Our sense of unworthiness leads us into passivity, which is defined in *Webster's Dictionary 1828* as "Suffering; not acting" and as "Unresisting; not opposing; receiving or suffering without resistance."[1] Passivity is doing nothing. The Bible tells us to take action: "Therefore submit to God. Resist the devil and he will flee from you" (James 4:7). Conquering our deliverance process depends on actively resisting the devil. We cannot just resist him in certain areas; we need to resist him in all areas.

Passivity detours Christians from their destiny and keeps them in bondage. You have to work your way through your deliverance; you cannot be set free by doing nothing. You break inactivity by rising up and doing something about it. You must fight the passivity spirit in the natural. To do that, you get up and pray and war against it, even when you don't feel like it. It is praying audibly and declaring against your situation.

Passivity is a difficult spirit to fight because it paralyzes us into not wanting to do anything about our situation. Or we may want to do something about it, but we don't know how to fight at that

1. *American Dictionary of the English Language: Webster's Dictionary 1828*, s.v. "Passive," http://webstersdictionary1828.com/Dictionary/passive.

level, so we stay in what I call false contentment, which means settling for what is, rather than pressing on into what could be.

Passivity is a binding spirit that makes you numb. Instead of succumbing to those feelings, you need to get active. The Bible says that "the kingdom of heaven suffers violence, and the violent take it by force" (Matthew 11:12). I like the way the Modern English Version reads: "The kingdom of heaven has forcefully advanced, and the strong take it by force."

Change how you see yourself. See yourself as strong. Find the warrior within. Rise up and fight. Take it by force. Resist feelings of passivity and unworthiness. Do something about your situation!

Press Through to Breakthrough

People who feel unworthy are complacent and passive about receiving inner healing and deliverance. They don't always want to face issues from which they need healing. It requires work to focus on dealing with their faults and failures, which means they cannot stay inactive. The healing process also can bring up more feelings of unworthiness, another reason for them to avoid it.

Passivity can be as simple as not pressing in. It masks itself as false contentment. Along with being content with what God has given us, shouldn't we always want more? I want more! I want more of His presence and power. I want to become better equipped and have more material possessions so I can give more to His Kingdom.

We cannot settle. There was a time in my life when I was content. My ministry was good. I had not yet seen some prophetic words manifest and had accepted that perhaps they never would. Then God sent a prophet into my life who prophesied to the exact word the prophecies I had already figured might not manifest. He repeated word for word what God had told me in my secret place. It made me discontent. I realized I had settled. I went to God in prayer and said, *God, I had accepted what I was doing and that perhaps my ministry wouldn't grow any further. Why did You bring that word forth and make me discontent?*

God responded, *Kathy, if you are content, you won't press in for more. I don't want you content.*

This particular prophecy was long, but I decided no longer to be content with not seeing its manifestation. By taking action and decreeing and declaring its fulfillment, I saw two pieces of that prophetic word manifest only six weeks after it was released.

Physical Passivity

Through physical tiredness and lack of ambition, passivity affects our Christian walk. We were created to worship, pray, study our Bible and accomplish some specific things for the Kingdom. God made each of us with destiny in mind. He may have given you instructions to start a Christian business, write a book or learn a new instrument to worship Him. You get home from work tired, however, or you fill your day with unnecessary busyness and errands that wear you down, or you simply waste time. Your body gets tired and fatigued, so that by the end of the day you make up excuses for not pressing in to the things of the Lord or spending time in His presence. Because emotionally you don't want to press in, your excuses come out as *I'm tired physically*, or *I just got home from a long day.*

You have to move the excuses out of the way. Don't you think Jesus was tired carrying that cross? But He kept carrying it. What would have happened if Jesus had been passive? What if He had given up? We would not have available to us salvation, healing, deliverance and our victory. When you don't feel like being obedient to what God is calling you to and you don't feel like doing anything, you need to remember that Jesus pressed through. You owe it to Him to press through, too.

If you are tired when you get home from work, take a fifteen-minute nap and then get up and get going. Take care of your body to bring it strength by exercising, eating healthy and drinking water. Your body gets tired when you need protein, so make sure you count protein grams and get the required amount. In Bible times, they did not stop working after an eight-hour day; they went from sunup to sundown. Don't make excuses. Get physically, emotionally and spiritually fit to advance the Kingdom of God.

Passivity and Prayerlessness

Passivity causes prayerlessness. We don't pray because we don't know what to say, or we feel we are repetitive in our prayer time. We don't pray because we are tired. Excuses come forth because again, we don't know how to press through to our breakthrough, and a spirit of paralysis is keeping us bound in our old ways.

When you are stuck in a dry spot in your prayer life, it is challenging to revive it. Praying audibly is one way to revive your prayer life and break off passivity. It takes less effort to pray in our mind, connecting spirit to spirit with God, but this can also lead to thinking or pondering, when we really need to be praying. Praying in our mind can then lead to passivity, whereas praying out loud prevents this.

I instruct people to speak out their prayers. The Bible instructs us about the power of our outspoken words and tells us that "death and life are in the power of the tongue" (Proverbs 18:21). In my book *Speak Out*, I discuss how Jesus and the Father spoke out all the time. We should follow Jesus' example of prayer and also be praying audibly. You cannot fall asleep or be passive in your prayer time when you are declaring out loud.

What would happen if all Christians started praying audibly? There is too much passivity in our prayer life. Think about it. You start praying, *Heavenly Father, please do this, and please do that. God, I need this, and I need that.* What happens? Your prayers are boring, so you fall asleep. Your prayer life is not doing anything for you, so you stop praying. But if we would rise up and exude the power of our words with force, we could bring forth change.

What is it going to hurt to try praying differently? Get up and ignite your prayer life by commanding and decreeing. Speak this out:

In the name of Jesus, I command blessings today. I command the heavens to open. I command things in my life to change. I bind and restrict the devil from attacking me, in Jesus' name. I command all demonic assignments to break, in Jesus' name. I speak and declare that I am called and chosen by the Lord, and I will arise and take my rightful place and position in the Kingdom of God. I will be a dangerous weapon against the enemy. Passivity and unworthiness will no longer bind me, in Jesus' name. Amen!

If you did not repeat that out loud, then right now stop reading and speak it aloud as though you mean it. You may have to declare it three times or more. Declare it until you mean it and feel something break in the spiritual realm.

The more you pray like this, the more you are not going to want to leave your prayer time once you start. But you have to get over that initial hurdle. What happens when you start exercising? You cough, you get tired and you can't go on. I remember that when I first started running, I always hit that hurdle. For me, it was about 12 minutes in when I would think, *Man, if I could just press through to 13, 14 and 15 minutes!* I knew that if I reached minute 15, I would be able to run as long as I wanted.

That is what you have to do with your prayer life. You have to pray until you get past that hurdle. You have to pray in faith. You have to pray until the anointing kicks in. Once that anointing kicks in, you won't want to stop praying, because heaven has opened and you are having so much fun. The Holy Spirit has descended upon you and is simply praying through you.

Characteristics of Passive People

Passive people don't know how to stand up for themselves, and they avoid confrontation. They don't want to confront others, because confrontation may lead to a disagreement that upsets them and feeds back into their unworthiness.

Passivity that avoids conflict at all costs causes dissension in marriages and families. One parent could be the disciplinarian, while the other sits by and criticizes how things are done. The criticizing parent, who is passive, does not want to take an active role or be the disciplinarian because that leads to conflict, which he or she wants to avoid at all costs.

Passive people will settle instead of trying to improve themselves. Even though they are discontent, they will not put in the effort required to go the next mile in improving themselves or their situation, for fear of failure. This can include people who need to find a better job or ask for a raise. Fear of failure will have them settling at home in poverty, instead of applying for employment or asking for a wage increase.

Passive people will procrastinate. When it comes to yard work, car repairs or whatever else needs to be done or maintained around the house, a passive person will think of these things as requiring great effort. They will make things seem like a mountain instead of a molehill. Then the laziness and excuses they operate in will prevent the necessary things from getting done.

Just as passivity can be an issue in our lives today, we see examples of it throughout the Bible. It has shown up throughout history, but we must come against it in our own lives. We have to root it out. The attitude and victim mentality that "it is not my responsibility, and someone else will do it" must go.

I don't want to make someone else do the job God sent me to do. "For many are called, but few are chosen" (Matthew 22:14). I want to be chosen. I don't want to lose my assignment. I don't want to get tired and discouraged, as Elijah did, and want to give up (see 1 Kings 19). Elijah had to anoint Elisha as a prophet in his place.

Deliverance from passivity starts by saying, *God, I repent of a passive spirit. I repent of doing nothing.* We need to become a repentant generation. Repentance breaks bondages. Repentance is when we come to God and say, *God, forgive me.* And we pray for the strength we need to persevere. I used to hate exercising, so I prayed and cried out, *God, give me a love for exercise.* I now run and walk to keep physically fit for the Kingdom, and I enjoy doing both!

We need to become desperate for our deliverance. We need to cry out to God to convict us and expose the strongholds in our lives. My saying is, *God, peel back the layers of me as we would peel back an onion, until there is nothing left of me, and there is all of You.* Allowing God to remove the layers is allowing Him to remove areas of emotional trauma and sin.

Sin Shouldn't Hold You Back

The disciples sinned, yet Jesus used them. We have to remove the guilt, condemnation and regret of the past. Remember at the beginning of the chapter how I told you that because of my sins, I did not feel as if I were good enough to be a pastor's wife? Now look at how God is using me!

I am sure if we could speak to our former self, there are some things we would change about decisions we made. We cannot go back, so our only choice is to move forward. Look what the Bible says about our past:

> Brethren, I do not count myself to have apprehended; but one thing I do, forgetting those things which are behind and reaching forward to those things which are ahead, I press toward the goal for the prize of the upward call of God in Christ Jesus.
>
> Philippians 3:13–14

> Do not remember the former things, nor consider the things of old.
>
> Isaiah 43:18

I have been crucified with Christ; it is no longer I who live, but Christ lives in me; and the life which I now live in the flesh I live by faith in the Son of God, who loved me and gave Himself for me.

Galatians 2:20

Therefore, if anyone is in Christ, he is a new creation; old things have passed away; behold, all things have become new.

2 Corinthians 5:17

If we confess our sins, He is faithful and just to forgive us our sins and to cleanse us from all unrighteousness.

1 John 1:9

What Defines Our Worth

Our self-worth is not defined by the sins we have committed. It is defined by who we are in Christ. People have allowed their self-worth to be defined by the happenings of life and the words spoken to them. Hearing words such as *you're no good, no one will ever love you,* or *you aren't going to succeed in life* are harmful to our self-image. When we hear them as children and have not yet been taught how to rebuke those thoughts, we don't know how to deny them entry. Instead, we believe the negative words. Negative words spoken over us don't need to define us anymore. We are made in God's image, and we have a Father who loves us. He will never speak negatively over us.

Do you have low self-worth because your parents told you as a child that you would never amount to anything? You are living as a product of your past, but you don't have to stay there. You can renew your mind to remove the lies and negative remarks your parents or other people spewed over you in anger. Words hurt, and all those words accumulate, causing us to think less of ourselves. But hurting people hurt people. When people say things that we take in as hurt and pain, it is because they are hurting and don't know how to receive healing from their own hurt. Out of that pain, people will say things that tear other people down.

As children and even as adults, we have all taken in some negative words. Buried within us over the years, those words have then built strongholds in our lives. By keeping them buried, we keep ourselves in prison to our past abuse, neglect, rejection, abandonment and self-worth issues.

Yet our self-worth is not based on ourselves, or on what we have done, or on what people have done to us. It is based on who we are in and through Jesus Christ. God created us in His image. What does that mean? We are worthy. We are justified. We are righteous. We are beautiful. We are loved. We are wanted. You and I know who we are by what the Word of God says about us: "And the LORD will make you the head and not the tail; you shall be above only, and not be beneath" (Deuteronomy 28:13).

Christians often feel unworthy because they don't know how to accept the Father's love. They relate to their heavenly Father the same way they relate to their earthly father. But your heavenly Daddy is not like anyone else. He loves you! He wants you! He isn't going to treat you the way your earthly daddy did; He is going to treat you much better!

Do you feel accepted and loved by Jesus? What if He walked into the room right now, took some oil, stroked your face and said, "You are worthy and loved"?

Would you tremble in fear, saying, "No, Lord, don't touch me"? Or would you smile and embrace Him, accepting His words of praise and saying, "Yes, Lord, I know"? As we look at and deal with our issues related to unworthiness, we can all get to a place of saying, "Yes, Lord, I know!"

Can You Receive?

This question may not appear related to unworthiness, but I want to ask you, Can you receive? Can you receive when a person wants to buy you coffee or pay your bill at mealtime? Or do you go back and forth, saying, "No, I'll pay"? Can you receive a gift when a person brings you a present, or do you respond with, "You didn't have to get me anything"?

Being unable to receive can be due to unworthiness. A victim or poverty mentality can have us believing that we don't deserve blessings. Low self-esteem makes us think good things are never going to happen to us. It is great if you like to give, and you can justify your gift giving to others by saying, "I like to be the giver of gifts, and being blessed doesn't matter that much to me." But you also need to learn to receive. You need to receive so the other person can be blessed by God. The gift, meal or blessing you are receiving is not from that person; it is from God!

God told me once, *Kathy, if you can't receive a cup of coffee from someone, how are you going to receive the larger blessings I want to give you?* God needs to teach us that we are worthy to receive little things, so that when we receive the larger things we are not completely overwhelmed.

Is your argument that you don't need gifts or blessings? What if God wants you to have them? What if He wants to bless you so you can distribute those blessings upon the earth? Do this exercise before you continue reading: Sit silently for a few minutes and ask the Holy Spirit if you have a problem receiving. And then receive whatever He has to say.

Deep down inside, we all want to receive and be blessed. The challenge is that we don't know how. It is a learning process. I, too, had a problem receiving. The Lord used many people to bless me and help me overcome the problem. Now I like receiving gifts. In fact, it has become my love language. I like having people offer to buy me a latte, or having them just show up at a meeting with a hot drink to hand me. I enjoy receiving gifts, and it does not matter if it is a dollar store gift or an expensive present. I love receiving all gifts!

Physical Appearance and Self-Worth

Your physical appearance does not define you. Can you look in the mirror and say, "I love myself"? Can you say that and really mean it, despite what the mirror reflects back to you? Can you look in the mirror and love yourself regardless of your physical body? Can you love yourself even with your curves and bulges? Can you stand naked in front of the mirror and say, "I love what I see"?

We need to love ourselves for who we are, despite our physical appearance. We are not to love ourselves based on our physical body, but based on our emotional and spiritual selves. Our society makes this difficult since one of the things this world bases self-worth on is physical appearance. The beauty industry says the better we look, the more we are valued. God cares about the matters of the heart. He tells us not to show partiality or define people by their outward appearance:

> For if there should come into your assembly a man with gold rings, in fine apparel, and there should also come in a poor man in filthy clothes, and you pay attention to the one wearing the fine clothes and say to him, "You sit here in a good place," and say to the poor man, "You stand there," or, "Sit here at my footstool," have you not shown partiality among yourselves, and become judges with evil thoughts?

> James 2:2–4

Outward appearances do not make up our self-worth. Society is critical and judgmental regarding people's outward appearance, thinking it defines who they are inside. It does not, even though it is biblical to eat healthy, exercise and take care of our temples, our physical bodies. Where we go overboard is when we passively do nothing to improve our condition, or when we become obsessed with our outward appearance and our body becomes an idol.

I was taught growing up that you put on makeup, do your hair every day and make sure you don't become a slouchy housewife.

(Although I am writing this right now with my husband at home and me in my pj's, with no makeup on and a hat on my head to cover up my messy hair.) Later, as a speaker, I was trained to look at myself and ask, *Would someone want to look at this for six hours?* People even define me as a "girly girl." I don't see that myself, but that's what I hear. I wear nice clothes, have my hair and nails done, like makeup and love wearing jewelry. But none of this prep work on my physical being defines me. It does not make me feel better about myself. It does not determine my inward value.

I do not wear jewelry to get attention, either, or to make myself look rich. In fact, I get a thrill out of telling people how inexpensively I purchase my real (not costume) jewelry. I wear real jewelry because my husband likes to show his love for me with it, and I think it's pretty. I love jewelry. I can adorn myself with jewels, but it does not make me feel rich or make me feel better on a bad day.

Even though I am a girly girl, I have not always felt secure about my physical self. Because I was carrying a few extra pounds, I did not think I could dance in worship before the Lord. But God told me, *I don't care what size you are if you want to dance before Me. You are beautiful in My eyes.*

I do believe we should try to achieve an ideal body weight and glorify God with our eating. Yes, I am finally there! But until we get there, God knows our heart and loves us just the same. Finding freedom in worship is not just for people with a few extra pounds. There are people who are physically fit but don't feel they can dance before the Lord, because they have not had dance lessons. You don't need dance lessons; just start dancing before Him.

A Word for Women

If you are a man, I know I have been talking to women about jewelry and makeup, but bear with me while I deal with a couple more things with the ladies. Your makeup does not define you! There are women who literally cannot go out of the house without makeup. I have known women who would get up early, even while traveling, to put on makeup before anyone else woke up. Another woman I know stopped participating in certain events because she would always cry, and it messed up her makeup.

I used to be one of those women who could not go out of the house without makeup. Now, I work in the office and go to the store plain faced on occasion, and if my team or the people to whom I minister see me, oh well. I even made my team go out on the streets of Las Vegas and minister to the homeless without makeup. I told them they had five minutes to get out on the streets. Some of them tried to cram makeup on before they walked out the door, but in five minutes they could not do it. They thanked me when they got in from doing evangelism, however. They said it made them more real, and it made it easier to relate to the people they met who were not wearing makeup.

Our clothes may make us feel good or confident, but they should not define us. Our identity can get caught up in our attire, especially on Sundays at church. You can feel as if you are dressed for success, but it cannot mask the internal pain you suffer. You can experience a spurt of joy because you look great, but inside, you are the same person. Do you want people to compliment your clothes, hair and makeup, or do you want them to compliment your spirit person? The highest compliment I can get is when people want to be around me because they love being around Jesus in me.

We often measure our self-worth based on our career, status and achievements. We think, *If I am successful, then I am worthy.* Perhaps to the world that is true, but not to our God. In fact, the majority of rich, successful people don't feel a need for God because they feel they can do it on their own.

I can run a successful ministry, write, preach and cast out demons, but it still does not make me worthy. I can be an author, travel the world and have people admire me, but when I come home at the end of the day, I will still be me. And I know the one who defines me and makes me feel worthy is Jesus.

Appearances change, jewelry breaks and gets lost and stolen, makeup washes off, clothes wear out, jobs come and go and bank accounts empty. What is left? You! Only bare-naked you! You better establish your self-worth and know who you are in Christ, because sometimes all you have left is bare-naked you. Divorces happen, people die, homes get foreclosed, cars crash and natural disasters cause us to lose everything. And what is left? Only bare-naked you. I hope you begin to like you!

From Pauper to Royalty

Look at the story of Esther. She was nothing and became a queen. She went from pauper to royalty. She went from rags to riches. She saved her people. She spent a year preparing to be presented to the king. She studied him and wanted to know about him and what he liked.

What are you doing to prepare for King Jesus? What are you doing to break off your pauper mentality and realize that you are royalty? How are you cleaning up your soul and preparing to serve Him now and spend eternity with Him?

In one year the Lord showed me and made me believe I am a princess. He had to remove my pauper, victim mentality and turn it into royalty. My immediate family started purchasing crown items for me for that year's Mother's Day. They pampered me, cooked, cleaned, gave me a pedicure and a foot massage and made my favorite dessert. They always treat me well on Mother's Day, but this day was different. The Lord continued to transition my thinking about who I was in Him through the gift of prophecy. He had some people prophesy over me (which is giving words of encouragement) four times in one day. All the people who prophesied, who could not hear each other and did not know what the others said, released words over my life about being a princess.

In this same transitional season, I was ministering with other leaders and performing water baptisms. In the middle of my conversation with one of them, she reached around her neck and took off a crown necklace. She said, "God wants you to have this. It's not real; I wish it were, for you. It's one of my most prized possessions, and God wants you to have it." God has used crown symbols in my ministry in powerful ways and still does today.

The story of the prodigal is a wonderful story of how people should be treated (see Luke 15:11–24). The lost son did not feel worthy, but his father made him feel worthy. That is how we should treat other people and ourselves. This story says, "Despite everything, I'm going to treat you like royalty." This father gave his son a break. Our heavenly Father is saying the same thing to you and me. But it starts with us giving ourselves a break and forgiving ourselves, and with releasing offenders of the offenses they have committed against us.

In Luke 7:1–10, when the centurion came and asked Jesus for healing, the man felt unworthy. Yet Jesus considered him worthy. This man had soldiers under his authority. He was a commander, a person in charge, yet he felt unworthy. But Jesus' treatment of him said *you are worthy!* God will do for you what He did for the centurion.

We lack in our preparations for the Kingdom of God. We don't know we are royalty, seated in heavenly places. We don't realize we have an inheritance that we can begin to live out now. We have not been prepared for becoming royalty, and have not been taught our value in Christ.

Moses was born to lead the Israelites out of slavery. Before that happened, he had to be raised in Pharaoh's house so that he would learn how to be a prince and not have a slave mentality. A leader who is enslaved internally cannot free those who are enslaved externally. We need to transition our thinking. We need to get rid of our pauper, victim mentality, which can form through generational curses and from the way we were raised and taught. We cannot begin to accomplish what the Lord has for us until we know the value He has placed on our lives.

Walking Out Your Deliverance

You may need to renew your mind and ignore negative words people have spoken over you and to you. Discover who you are and whose you are by knowing your identity in Christ. Remember always that you are worthy because Christ is worthy and lives in you. Allow that truth to become a reality and manifestation in your soul.

Scriptures on Identity

John 1:12; Romans 8:1, 17; 1 Corinthians 6:17; 2 Corinthians 5:17; Galatians 2:20; Ephesians 1:5; Philippians 3:20

Prayer of Repentance and Forgiveness

Pray this prayer audibly to repent and release forgiveness:

Heavenly Father, in the name of Jesus, Your Son, my Lord and Savior, I willfully give up these spirits of passivity, complacency, laziness, slumber and disobedience!

In the name of Jesus, I take authority over and remove all gossip, slander, negativity and false accusations spoken against me or about me. I command every demonic assignment against my family and me to be null and void, in Jesus' name. Every territorial, familiar, generational, hereditary and genealogy spirit, I cancel your assignment and cover myself and my family with the blood of Christ.

I thank You, Jesus, that You were cursed for me, and therefore every curse against my life is broken. I receive the freedom You purchased for me and my family line at the cross.

Devil, I'm speaking to you! Get under my feet; you will hinder me no more. I'm claiming, commanding and decreeing for passivity to break off and loose its chains from my family, my ministry and myself, in the mighty name of Jesus!

Father, forgive me for feeling unworthy of Your love and unworthy to be used by You. I ask that You show me my identity and who I am in Christ. I know You have made me in Your image; therefore, I am equipped with every good thing. I forgive myself for these feelings of insecurity and inadequacy, and I ask You to change me, in Jesus' name. Amen.

Spirits to Discern and Cast Out

Ask the Holy Spirit to reveal all the demonic spirits associated with unworthiness and passivity that you need to cast out. Out loud, command these spirits to leave: "Spirit of _____, go, in Jesus' name!" You may have to do this several times over a period of time. Do it until you feel peace, a release or a spiritual shift. Spirits often associated with unworthiness and passivity:

Abandonment, Ahab, attention, bondage, complacency, critical, deep hurt, depression, despair, discontent, discouragement, distrust, doubt, failure, fear, fear of confrontation, heaviness, hopelessness, humiliation, inadequacy, insecurity, intimidation, laziness, loneliness, mind binding, passivity, self-condemnation, self-hate, self-pity, shame, slothful, slumbering, unworthiness, victim mentality, woundedness

Prayer of Activation

Heavenly Father, I receive Your love and know that I will arise and be the person You have created me to be. I thank and praise You that from this day forward, I'm going to be a world changer. I'm going to be different. I'm not going to settle, because Christ does not want me to settle. He has greater; He has more; He has victory! I want that victory!

I thank You, Jesus, that I am worthy because You are worthy and live in me. I call forth self-worth, love, acceptance and joy. I say and decree that I have peace of mind and the mind of Christ.

177

I thank You, Father, that Your Son, Jesus, died on the cross to make these feelings of inadequacy go to the grave. I receive the love, forgiveness and equipping that You have for me so I can accomplish Your Kingdom tasks. I call forth that I will be effective and useful for the Kingdom, and that I will walk in and manifest my full calling and destiny. I say that I have useful and creative ideas for the Kingdom. I will prosper in the very thing You have sent me for and designed for me, in Jesus' name. Amen!

Declarations to Speak Out

Speak out the following faith declarations and spiritual warfare declarations. Bookmark these pages and come back to them as often as necessary to assist you in renewing your mind, transforming your heart and increasing your faith.

Faith Declarations

Make these faith declarations audibly, with power and authority, believing that you will receive them. Speak them out from a position of *I have these*, not *I'm trying to obtain these*. While you transition from unworthiness to self-worth and from passivity to action, read these declarations out regularly to help you grow strong in faith and renew your mind.

- I rebuke and renounce a victim mentality. I am not defeated. I am victorious.
- I will be active in my faith. I will arise and shine, for the glory of the Lord is upon me.
- I will take my rightful place and position in battle to advance the Kingdom of God.
- Powers of darkness will not invade me, making me feel and think that I am weak. When I feel weak, I know that through God I am made strong.

- I have a purpose and a calling to complete for the Kingdom of God.
- I love to move and be active for the Kingdom and in my life.
- My physical appearance does not define who I am; Jesus does!
- I do not need worldly garments in order to think I am beautiful. I have a Father in heaven who loves me just as I am.
- I am not a defeated foe. The enemy cannot weigh me down, because the joy of the Lord is my strength, in Jesus' name.

Spiritual Warfare Declarations

Make these spiritual warfare declarations audibly, with power and authority. When you speak out these declarations, you are taking up your God-given authority to bind and restrict the enemy and counteract future attacks. Declare them repeatedly, until you feel something release in the spiritual atmosphere.

- I bind and restrict all mind-binding spirits and declare that you will not torment me, making me think I am less than who I am.
- I penetrate the powers of darkness and speak and declare that I am worthy because Jesus is worthy and lives in me!
- I have resurrection power. The same power that raised Jesus from the dead lives in me; therefore, I have strength. I am strong in the Lord.
- I command every dart of the enemy that tries to attack my mind not to attack. I am not lowly, but I am high and lifted up, seated in heavenly places in the spiritual realm.
- I declare that my identity comes from Christ and is in Christ.
- No inadequate thinking can come my way. My mind is renewed!

- I put a hedge of protection around my mind, and I put on the helmet of deliverance to guard my thoughts and keep my mind from thinking negatively about myself.
- I command all self-hate, unworthiness and passivity to get out of my life, in Jesus' name.

CHAPTER 10

VICTIM AND POVERTY MENTALITIES

Self-Assessment Test—Spirit of Victim or Poverty Mentality

On a scale of 1 to 10, rate each statement below.

1. Negative thoughts plague my mind.
2. I often feel defeated, worn down and heavy-hearted.
3. I feel that no matter how hard I attempt to gain financially, I meet resistance.
4. I feel abandoned, alone and as if no one cares.
5. There are times I feel as though people are not truly hearing what I have to say or are not interested in listening.
6. I feel I have nothing of value to give, emotionally or physically.
7. I try to change my thoughts in a victorious direction, but feel stuck in a cycle of defeat.

There were times in my life when I felt like a victim mentally when it came to issues in my finances. More than once, God called us to give up our home and employment for ministry reasons. Even though we had the faith to trust Him through those times, I would be lying if I said I never felt defeated and worried about finances. When we looked for a home after we had left one pastorate, Ron's paycheck said owning one would be impossible for us. But as we walked through a certain home, we knew God wanted us to have it, so we trusted Him.

There were times when I knew that I genuinely should not buy things, so I held off and did not even grab a latte or order a pizza. I withheld spending money when I knew expenditures were not in our best financial interest. There were other times, however, when I could have afforded to purchase something, but I did not because I still had a poverty/victim mentality. I had to work for years to overcome those thoughts in my mind and get past how I had been raised to think like a pauper instead of a child of God with a heavenly inheritance.

For a long time, my mind was bound in lack and I focused on what I did not have, when instead, I could have been using the power of my words to release what I could have. There were times I would worry and feel defeated. I was not trusting God as my provider, even though we never lacked or went without. When we are in lack, one of the ways we break that lack is by becoming a giver:

But this I say: He who sows sparingly will also reap sparingly, and he who sows bountifully will also reap bountifully. So let each one give as he purposes in his heart, not grudgingly or of necessity; for God loves a cheerful giver. And God is able to make all grace abound toward you, that you, always having all sufficiency in all things, may have an abundance for every good work.

2 Corinthians 9:6–8

Generosity Looses Deliverance

Giving has a natural and spiritual correlation. It is taking something natural and carnal (money) and turning it into something spiritual. When you give, you are taking a material possession or your monetary gain and turning it into something spiritual that builds the Kingdom of God. When you give to God, you are sowing into other people and allowing change to penetrate their lives.

In Old Testament times, God's people consistently gave to Him by slaughtering animals and making sacrifices. Thankfully, we don't have to do that kind of giving today, but we still need to give. It does good both for us and for the recipients. Look at Malachi 3:8–11:

> "Will a man rob God? Yet you have robbed Me! But you say, 'In what way have we robbed You?' In tithes and offerings. You are cursed with a curse, for you have robbed Me, even this whole nation. Bring all the tithes into the storehouse, that there may be food in My house, and try Me now in this," says the LORD of hosts, "If I will not open for you the windows of heaven and pour out for you such blessing that there will not be room enough to receive it.
>
> "And I will rebuke the devourer for your sakes, so that he will not destroy the fruit of your ground, nor shall the vine fail to bear fruit for you in the field," says the LORD of hosts.

I love the fact that this passage says when we give to the Lord, He will rebuke the devourer for us. If we look at everything we have as a gift from God, we will realize that we can give it away because it really is His, not ours.

Changing our victim mentality to one of generosity will loose our deliverance. We need to have the mentality of *just give it away.* The Bible says, "Give, and it will be given to you: good measure, pressed down, shaken together, and running over will be put into your bosom. For with the same measure that you use, it will be measured back to you" (Luke 6:38).

Changing Our Words Changes Us

If we want to change our mentality, we need to change our words. "So then faith comes by hearing, and hearing by the word of God" (Romans 10:17). The more we speak out our words, the more we will believe them. And as we believe them, we will receive them.

Don't say, "I can't afford it." Get those words out of your vocabulary. When your child asks you for something in the store, simply say, "We're not choosing to spend our money on that right now." You don't want to transfer your poverty mentality or fear of lack to your kids. Don't create a generational curse by continually saying to your children, "We can't afford that." What I used to say was, "We're waiting for our financial blessing to manifest."

I trained our children by using proper wording about our finances. When we were in a store and one of my daughters wanted something, she would therefore ask, "Mommy, when our financial blessing manifests, may I have this?"

Once, I felt the Lord leading me to give away our van. We could have gotten $600 for it on a trade-in. Although all our needs were met, we could have used that $600. When I told my husband about the van, he asked, "Are you serious? You want to give the van away?"

I answered, "Yes!" Keeping the $600 was not worth walking in disobedience to God. Over the years after giving it away, God enabled us to buy three different vans for $6,000 each, and they all worked great. God even gave us a triple return on our investment when three of our immediate family members all received free vehicles within five days of each other.

A Victim Mentality

People with a victim mentality will often complain about what they don't have. They exude signs of *feel sorry for me*, and *if you know my need, maybe you'll supply it*. We must trust God, not people, as our provider, even though He will use people.

I remember one time when I needed a washing machine, but I did not tell anyone. One of my team members was down by my washer and made a comment about it, and I said, "Yes, I need to replace mine."

She responded, "My parents have an extra one I need to get rid of that you can have."

I had not gone around announcing, "My washer broke and I don't know how I'm going to afford a new one." I had not gone on and on in the defeat of a victim mentality to get people to feel sorry for me. When we are in need, often we do that as a way of speaking out our defeat and manipulating others to see if we can get the provision we need. Again, we need to trust God as our provider.

Experiencing feelings of defeat and having a victim mentality can affect more than just our finances. It can penetrate every area of our lives. When we get passed over and ignored, and we feel as if we are invisible and downtrodden, we can take on a defeated victim mentality. If we are hammered with frequent physical sickness and are always experiencing problems, we can feel defeated. But Jesus defeated the devil at the grave, and now we don't have to experience defeat. I believe that a lot of the time, we choose to feel defeated. We choose our reactions and feelings. We can make a choice to live as a victim or as a victor. What's your choice?

People who don't know how to turn their challenging situation around often feel defeated. They feel as if they are victims of their circumstances. You are not a victim! You are an heir to a royal throne, and you need to change your emotional reactions so you are acting as if nothing can touch you. I don't want to open a door to demonic infiltration of my soul, so when a spiritual attack comes, or when a person does something negative against me, I choose my response. I choose not to allow rejection, offense and bitterness to come into my heart, my soul and my temple. You can choose your response, too.

A victim mentality builds up because you have been humanly or spiritually attacked so many times that you don't arise and fight.

185

It is like taking blow after blow, always feeling as if the enemy is hammering you. The enemy is not always attacking you, however, and people are not always out to get you. A lot of the time, it is your perception and how you are reacting to a situation.

A victim mentality comes forth due to years of hurt you have piled up inside, and it opens a doorway to offense and rejection. When you have experienced a rough time in life, and things and relationships have not gone your way, you get tired and fatigued. Those emotions build up, and your escape is to talk out your feelings. As you talk them out to people, however, they can get tired of your sob stories and tired of hearing you complain. When they shut you down, you then feel rejected and offended. This leads to further feelings of defeat. You get stuck in a cycle that you don't know how to get out of.

Relationships may be a place where you have felt victimized, but the common factor in all your relationships is *you*. As difficult as it is to hear, everyone else can't be wrong all the time. You are the common denominator, and until you open your heart to realize there are some things inside *you* that need to change, you are continually going to experience woundedness. Yet you are a warrior, not the permanently wounded.

Wounded people who manifest a defeated victim mentality can exhibit two primary signs. One sign is that they can become overbearingly talkative. They will push conversations, running endlessly from person to person while trying to discover an answer to their problem. They will not be looking for the right answer, necessarily, but rather for the answer they want to hear. A second sign is that they act lowly and defeated. They draw back and sink more into themselves, wallowing in their self-pity.

Don't Identify with Defeat

Defeat can come forth in our workplace, church or community. Perhaps you think you have amazing talent in an area in which you still need to grow. You apply for a job or volunteer position, and you don't get it. After numerous rejections, you feel defeated.

Often, such rejections will leave us in a state where we don't even want to try anymore, not only for positions, but also in relationships. We tend to give up because it is not worth putting effort into a situation where we feel we will just be victimized again. This is a wrong expectation, and we need to rise above those feelings of defeat!

Defeat is about perception. The devil is defeated; we are not. Defeat is sometimes about how we mistakenly identify ourselves with it. A military person who has had an amputation is not defeated; he or she is victorious because of fighting for our country when many people would not. A young mother is not defeated when her spouse wants a divorce and leaves her with the children. A millionaire is not defeated when he or she loses it all and ends up in poverty. Military personnel are not amputees, women are not divorcees, and millionaires are not victims. We cannot and should not identify with our defeat.

You are a child of the Most High God; that is your identification in Christ. Your identity is not in your circumstances, life's happenings or outward appearances. No one can change who you are in Christ and who He designed you to be. You need to know your identity in Him. You need to know who He says you are. If someone approaches you and asks who you are, your answer should not be that you are a preacher, a doctor, a divorcée or an amputee. Your answer should be, "I'm a child of the Most High God, and I'm a Kingdom citizen!

We need to speak out against trying circumstances and what and who the world says we are, and we need to manifest who we want to be in Christ and how we need to gain victory through the power of our words. "We are more than conquerors through Him who loved us" (Romans 8:37).

How do you overcome feelings of defeat, woundedness and a victim or poverty mentality? You have to rise up and fight! Stand strong and pull on your spirit man. The spirit within you is empowered, not defeated.

The devil wants to leave your mind in a place of defeat, but you have to pull up into that place of victory. You cannot stay passive and pull yourself out. Get up and get moving!

Growing in your spiritual walk despite opposition, despite when you don't want to, is key to your victory. You need to be in the Word of God and be releasing declarative prayer. You need to elevate your intimate time with the Lord through worship. You are not defeated; you have the victory in Jesus!

Walking Out Your Deliverance

Change your mindset and mentality by learning to be a giver. Ask the Holy Spirit to convict you about giving. Go through your possessions and see what you have that you can give away. Replace your defeated victim mentality by reading Galatians and Ephesians, books in which you will discover more about who you are in Christ, and the inheritance you walk in. Read books on your identity and spend time renewing your mind. When you feel defeated, get up and worship, and remember who you are in Christ!

Scriptures on Overcoming

Matthew 6:26, 33; 11:28; John 10:10; 16:33; 2 Corinthians 9:8; Hebrews 13:5; 1 Peter 5:7

Prayer of Repentance and Forgiveness

Pray this prayer audibly to repent and release forgiveness:

Father, forgive me for the way I have spent my money unnecessarily. Remove the poverty mentality from my mind. I ask You to show me how to be wise with my money. Show me how to be a giver.

Holy Spirit, convict me to give! Renew my mind about how everything I have belongs to You. Help me know that I am victorious and not a victim. The devil has been defeated; therefore, I am no longer defeated.

Jesus, I ask Your forgiveness for the times when I have felt like a victim and have not manifested the victory You have already given me. Help me to change, in Your name. Amen!

Spirits to Discern and Cast Out

Ask the Holy Spirit to reveal all the demonic spirits associated with victim and poverty mentalities that you need to cast out. Out loud, command these spirits to leave: "Spirit of _____, go, in Jesus' name!" You may have to do this several times over a period of time. Do it until you feel peace, a release or a spiritual shift. Spirits often associated with victim and poverty mentalities:

Anxiety, defeat, fear, greed, lack, mammon, poverty, rejection, self-condemnation, shame, unworthiness, victim mentality, worry

Prayer of Activation

I thank You, Father, that I am rising above my situation. You say in Your Word that we are blessed to give. I choose to be a giver. I thank You that I have the riches of heaven at my disposal. I purpose in my heart and mind to change my thought patterns. When I am lonely and defeated, I will choose You as my comforter, guide and friend. Your companionship is what I need. Help me purpose in my heart to give, and help me see the importance of giving financially to Your Kingdom. Help me become a cheerful tither on all my possessions. God, I choose to move forward in You and through You, in Your Son Jesus' name. Amen!

Declarations to Speak Out

Speak out the following faith declarations and spiritual warfare declarations. Bookmark these pages and come back to them as often as necessary to assist you in renewing your mind, transforming your heart and increasing your faith.

Faith Declarations

Make these faith declarations audibly, with power and authority, believing that you will receive them. Speak them out from a position of *I have these*, not *I'm trying to obtain these*. While you transition from victim and poverty mentalities to being a victorious overcomer, read these declarations out regularly to help you grow strong in faith and renew your mind.

- I decree that I am not of the world's economy, but of the Kingdom's economy.
- I have the riches of heaven at my disposal.
- Everything I put my hand to will prosper.
- I command unexpected checks to come to me in the mail and unknown money to appear for me.
- I call forth an increase in my checkbook, savings accounts, earnings and investments, in Jesus' name.
- I command bills to be paid, debts to be reduced and favor to come my way in mortgage reduction.
- I call forth open heaven over my finances.
- I am a giver and more than a conqueror in Christ Jesus.
- God's plans for my life will go forth, and through it all, I will find unprecedented favor because I am a giver.
- I do not give only out of my abundance. I give out of what I have, because everything belongs to God.
- I proclaim this is my year of abundance, my year of release, in Jesus' name.

Spiritual Warfare Declarations

Make these spiritual warfare declarations audibly, with power and authority. When you speak out these declarations, you are taking up your God-given authority to bind and restrict the enemy and counteract future attacks. Declare them repeatedly, until you feel something release in the spiritual atmosphere.

- I declare and decree that I have not been given a spirit of defeat, victimization or woundedness.
- I proclaim that I am a child of God; therefore, devil, get away from me.
- I rupture the plans of the enemy against me. I will not be defeated!
- I command the spirit of poverty to depart from me, my family and my business, in Jesus' name.
- Devil, I'm speaking to you: Get out of my mind, get out of my life and get out of my finances, in Jesus' name.
- Dark operations and cohorts coming against my prophetic destiny, be removed from your targeted assignments, in Jesus' name.

CHAPTER 11

GRIEF AND LOSS

Self-Assessment Test—Spirits of Grief and Loss

On a scale of 1 to 10, rate each statement below.

1. When I talk about a past instance that was sad, it still brings up feelings of grief.
2. When I talk about a loved one who died years ago, I still get emotional.
3. I have suffered loss and am unclear about the direction and future God has for me.
4. I cannot forgive myself for my past mistakes and sins.
5. When loss happens and seasons of life change, I have difficulty moving forward.
6. I cry for long periods of time, leading to depression or heaviness.
7. I stuff my feelings of loss, sadness and frustration instead of talking about them.

We all go through seasons of loss and grief. What could have been? What should have been? Grief can manifest in many ways. It can result from a job loss, a death, a change in seasons, a job transfer or a move.

I remember when my daughter Amber went to college. On the way up to school, the Lord told me three times this was His will for her life. I had never been to a dorm. I was horrified at what I discovered. Small rooms, sharing your entire life for nine months with someone else in your bedroom, and what I felt were less appealing living arrangements for my daughter than I had hoped. Not truly terrible; it was a credible university! But it was not like what she was accustomed to at home. I was mortified that my daughter would be living in such a place. I cried all the way home, and off and on for a few days afterward, even though her moving out was a tremendous blessing that needed to happen in order for her to fully embrace the call of God on her life and the relationship Jesus desired to have with her.

When you experience loss, you need to allow yourself to grieve. Often, we stuff our feelings of loss and think crying is a sign of weakness. Perhaps as a child, you were told not to cry because people were looking at you. Or perhaps your family was in a high-profile position, and outwardly your parents always wanted you to appear happy. We often won't allow ourselves to cry and experience loss because of concern over what others will think, but we have to release those emotions inside us or they will destroy us.

My daughter Lauren recently got married and moved out. I remember grieving throughout this process. It was not the *I'm gaining a son* mentality. I had already gained him in my heart two years before the wedding. I was losing my best friend and prayer partner, my daughter, and I was losing her dog. Yes, the dog! We had never wanted a dog, and two years ago we prayed and the Lord confirmed that Lauren was to have a Golden Retriever, Nakota. He stole my heart with his big smile and floppy ears. So I was not just losing my daughter, with whom I had late-night chats; I was losing my buddy, the puppy dog. Nakota had helped me lose 25 pounds on all the walks we had taken, and he sits at my feet when I write (he is at my feet now; I get him two days a week).

When Lauren went on her honeymoon, I grieved and cried. I was sad at some of the losses I experienced around that time. I did not, however, stay stuck in sadness. I allowed myself to cry and grieve, and then I knew I had to move forward. Healthy grieving and emotional release will produce deliverance in our lives. When we take our loss and expand on it for weeks on end, however, or stew it around continuously in our minds, then it can and does become a demonic stronghold that needs to be cast out. We need to find a balance between healthy grieving and allowing grief to consume us and develop into more than it should be.

Sources of Grief and Loss

Grief and loss can come from many different situations. One can be our unmet expectations of our spouse, family and friends. We often hold people in high esteem and want them to develop the same spiritual hunger that we have. But when we don't see change manifest in their lives, we grieve because we know that if they would embrace Jesus and their healing and deliverance the way we do, they could break their strongholds. We experience disappointment and take false responsibility on ourselves, and when our expectations go unmet, we grieve.

Another way grief and loss can manifest in our lives is through someone else's sins or actions. I remember telling my children for years, "Be careful what you do and what decisions you make, because your actions and decisions affect all of us." An entire family can be affected by one member's actions and end up grieving the loss that comes as a result.

The intimate side of our marriage can be another place in which we suffer loss and grief. Pornography and masturbation are strongholds in both men and women. When a spouse discovers that his or her other half is being captured by perverse spirits and is engaging in unclean sexual acts like watching pornography, it feels like a form of adultery. Even though that other spouse has not actually performed a physical act, spiritually and emotionally the person has defiled himself or herself and has dishonored the marriage, which leads to grief and loss.

When we lose our possessions through a home invasion, or when we experience a natural disaster like a fire or tornado that destroys our home, we suffer grief and loss. Although a family who faces such a scenario can come out grateful for their own safety, it is still a season of adjustment as they close one chapter of their lives and begin another. Early on in our marriage, our house was broken into. The criminals stole our stereo, jewelry and many other objects. My husband was sickened over the fact that they had robbed him of his Minolta camera, which I had purchased for him as a wedding gift. We felt invaded that someone had rummaged through our home and belongings. We had to grieve what we had lost, but most of all, we had to face the loss of our ability to feel safe.

If you sit down and analyze your life, you will discover pockets of grief and loss from which you need healing. I never understood grief and loss until I lived through it. I have cried over both my daughters and the dog. Loss is when we cannot control who left our life or what happened to us, and grief is moving through the emotions of it. Notice that I said *moving* through the emotions of it, not staying stuck in it. The problem with grief is that often, we don't move through it; we stay caught in the moment. We have to recognize grief for what it is—feeling a loss—and move on.

A sense of loss can come from different things and can affect us differently. I remember a jewelry store slicing my wedding ring diamond to the point that I had to get a new one. My original ring was destroyed, and to make matters worse, when my husband took the only pieces salvageable, some emeralds in the band, and had them made into a necklace, it broke and fell off me about a year later. Losing the necklace, too, made it a double loss for me. Having a wedding ring blessed in front of God was important to me. As I was sitting in a seminar one day, however, the speaker was speaking about selling Tupperware, and somehow the topic of loss came up. She said about the thing she had lost, "The sentiment will be forever in my heart."

She was right. I could not focus on the loss and what I did not have; I needed to look at what I did have—a husband who cared enough to have my emerald pieces reset into another piece of jewelry to enjoy while I could. On our ten-year anniversary, we renewed our wedding vows with a brand-new ring so it could be blessed again. I now have double the sentiment inside my heart.

Moving Through Loss

Although we all experience loss, it is what we do with that loss that will define us. We cannot get stuck in it, but need to move through it. One way to move through loss is not to have any expectations of what the process will look like, how long it will take or how you will feel. Just allow yourself to grieve and release the emotion of loss instead of stuffing it. If you shut down and bury your feelings, they will come out eventually, even if it is years later. Meanwhile, they will cause you pain and discomfort.

One time, someone we knew lost an older child to a drunk driver. The loss also meant losing any hope of enjoying future grandchildren. This parent's grief was therefore magnified since grandparenting someday had been anticipated with great joy. Now the grieving parent was left with the thought, *What am I going to do with my life? I may never have any grandchildren.* The loss of future hopes and dreams came with the loss of the child. Shortly after the accident, this parent started planting a garden as grief therapy.

Therapy dogs are another means through which people can release their loss, grief and other emotions. I never really understood therapy dogs. Honestly, I didn't have compassion for people needing a pet until my daughter Lauren's dog, Nakota, came into my life. I now understand how a person with emotional ailments, depression, anxiety, grief and loss can take one look into a pair of big puppy-dog eyes and feel better. The love and comfort a dog can bring to a hurting person are remarkable.

Yet we also need to stay balanced and focused during our time of hurt and grief, and remember that God is our healer, not a pet. Even though pets can bring tremendous comfort through the amazing hugs we can give them and the neck scratches they love, our focus should be on the Lord because He will have no other idols before Him, not even a pet He created. Some people will say that a pet can bring you comfort that Jesus cannot, but we have to be careful not to get out of balance that way and idolize a pet over Jesus. Keep balanced during your time of grief. Focus on Jesus being your healer.

Without God, how do people get through the grief and loss they suffer? The only way to handle loss in any and all situations is through your faith in God. Your faith had better be strong, because all kinds of loss will come. When it does, you need to move through it, not get stuck there.

Believe for a Greater Outcome

I mentioned earlier that we suffered loss more than once when we gave up our home, income, insurance and employment to be in ministry. Actually, the Lord called us to do that four different times. One time, we gave up tens of thousands of dollars as we sold our new house six weeks after the 9/11 terrorist attacks. We moved, picked up our kids, moved again, went into ministry and then left the ministry. We gave up everything for the sake of the Lord. It cost our kids their friends, their home and their comfort.

Two of them lost educational skills in the process of moving so much. Our greatest loss, however, was the partial amputation of my husband's finger. He worked a job in transition for $10 an hour just to do anything to provide for his family. One day he got his hand stuck in a machine, and off went the top of his finger.

You may say, "It's only a finger. It wasn't his hand or leg." Yes, that's true. I think of the Boston Marathon terrorist attack victims or our military personnel, people who lost whole limbs. Again, I cannot comprehend the pain, suffering and trauma they went through. I praise God it was not worse for my husband, but to a preacher, part of a finger is a loss. To a person who preaches and teaches with his hands, who has people staring at his expressive hands as he ministers, it is a loss. Our faith also got us through, however. By faith we got out a newspaper with a date on it that was three days after his accident, and we took a picture of his finger right next to that date. Someday, when God supernaturally does a creative miracle within his body and his finger grows back, we will have the proof, witness and testimony of what our God did.

We handled Ron's physical loss by lining up our faith. Where do you need to line up your faith and believe in your God for an outcome greater than your loss? In the spiritual warfare attacks we all face. When the enemy comes to steal, kill and destroy (see John 10:10), and when we have had the rug pulled out from under our feet, what do we do in those moments? How do we handle those situations? I believe we handle them by the grace of God, and by leaning on and relying on our faith. We counter such attacks by not allowing them to get the best of us. We have to get back up on our feet. It requires that we pray on the offense and diligently seek the Lord for direction and for our next step. We cannot allow our losses to defeat us. Instead, we have to defeat the enemy continually, as Jesus did, and counterattack our losses through prayer. God is our vindicator.

Walking Out Your Deliverance

In the inner healing process of grieving a loss, there are some specific steps you can take to work through it, depending on your situation. As you go through this deliverance section, note that it applies to many different situations, but that I will cover the steps involved in dealing with the loss of a child separately, in a "Walking Out . . ." section of its own at the end of the chapter.

Scriptures on Joy

Psalm 3:3; 30:1–5; John 16:22; Romans 12:12

Prayer of Repentance and Forgiveness

Pray this prayer audibly to repent and release forgiveness.

Heavenly Father, please help me through grief and loss in a healthy and productive manner. Convict me, Holy Spirit, if my suffering goes beyond biblical guidelines in the release of these emotions. I forgive those who have caused me to suffer grief and loss through a personal experience, life tragedy or physical manifestation. I choose today to move forward in joy and end my season of mourning. I trust You, Lord, for my future, in Jesus' name. Amen!

Spirits to Discern and Cast Out

Ask the Holy Spirit to reveal all the demonic spirits associated with grief and loss (whether the loss of a child or some different loss) that you need to cast out. Out loud, command these spirits to leave: "Spirit of _____, go, in Jesus' name!" You may have to do this several times over a period of time. Do it until you feel peace, a release or a spiritual shift. Spirits often associated with grief and loss:

Anger, bitterness, disappointment, grief, offense, rage, unforgiveness

Prayer of Activation

Holy Spirit, I thank You that You are my comforter, counselor and friend. I ask that You be my friend through this healing process, and always. I need Your comfort and guidance. I thank You that You were there with me through this, and that You will continue to be there for me. Holy Spirit, have Your way with me.

Jesus, I believe You are the rock and foundation of my faith. Help me stand strong. I give You permission, Lord, to use this situation to help others avoid making the same mistakes as I have made. I trust You for my life and healing, in Your name. Amen!

Declarations to Speak Out

Speak out the following faith declarations and spiritual warfare declarations. Note that I have included declarations for all kinds of grief and loss in general, and then also specifically for grief associated with the loss of a child. Bookmark these pages and come back to them as often as necessary to assist you in renewing your mind, transforming your heart and increasing your faith.

Faith Declarations for Grief and Loss

Make these faith declarations audibly, with power and authority, believing that you will receive them. Speak them out from a position of *I have these*, not *I'm trying to obtain these*. While you transition from grief and loss to healing and peace, read these declarations out regularly to help you grow strong in faith and renew your mind.

- I declare and decree that I am entering a new season of victory.
- I thank You, Lord, that You replace mourning with joy.

- I trust You, Holy Spirit, to help me move through seasons of loss in a healthy and productive way.
- I proclaim that I will put on a garment of praise for a spirit of heaviness.
- I declare that I will not stuff my emotions, but will allow myself to grieve through the seasons of life.
- I call forth that every good and perfect thing is coming my way.
- I command sadness and depression not to attack my emotions when traumas happen to me.
- I proclaim that my emotions are healthy, balanced and stable, in Jesus' name.

Spiritual Warfare Declarations for Grief and Loss

Make these spiritual warfare declarations audibly, with power and authority. When you speak out these declarations, you are taking up your God-given authority to bind and restrict the enemy and counteract future attacks. Declare them repeatedly, until you feel something release in the spiritual atmosphere.

- I proclaim that I am a child of the King and that no weapon formed against me, my children, my home and my finances will prosper.
- I bind, rebuke and cast out any and all attacks that would result in the destruction of my property or possessions.
- Devil, I am speaking to you. Get your hands off my family. You cannot have my children, spouse or loved ones. I bind and restrict demonic action against them.
- I decree and declare that death will not come prematurely to my family members.
- I bind and rebuke the enemy from stealing, killing and destroying anything and everything that is important to me.

- I rescind every demonic order that would cause me grief, pain and loss. I decree and declare and bind and restrict demonic attacks that will affect me.
- I annihilate every dark power from infiltrating my soul. My soul is whole and well balanced.
- I proclaim that I will live in victory and overcome any and all circumstances that are thrown my way, in Jesus' name.

Losing a Child

The loss of a child is extremely painful, so I want to look at it separately, and I want to preface this section by saying my heart goes out to all the parents who have lost a child in death after the child was born. (We will talk about the loss of an unborn child as well.) I do not even pretend to know the extreme loss and grief such parents have experienced.

I truly hope that if you have ever experienced the loss of a child, you will one day find the solace only God can provide. Also, note that while I am not discrediting the severe grief of losing a child of any age, this section is geared toward losing a child before he or she is born. This can happen through miscarriage or abortion. So many parents have not yet received healing after losing an unborn child in one of these ways. I have traveled the United States and ministered to thousands of women, and I am still amazed at the deep scars, regrets, pain and agony many women who have had an abortion are suffering. Until they walk through the healing process, their grief is a raw emotion from which they will suffer. I am well aware that many men have also suffered from losing an unborn child, and these men also need healing. For ease of writing, I will refer to women here, but if you are a man, please feel free to adapt whatever applies so that you, too, may receive healing.

No two people experience and handle loss the same way. Each person handles loss individually, according to how he or she processes the emotions of grief. When I went to the doctor and found out I was miscarrying, I handled it differently than some others I know of who also experienced that kind of loss. I felt I had to drive home first, before going to the hospital, so I could hold my other son in my arms. I cried and mourned in the process. Even today, everything in me would want my lost unborn son alive and with me. I think about him. God has shown me visions of him in heaven.

There are couples who experience miscarriage and are devastated. Losing a baby rocks their world in a negative sense, and they struggle to get through the loss. I have witnessed ladies going into depression and having to seek counseling to get through the emotional pain.

Everyone processes grief and loss differently. When I minister to people suffering loss, I usually say, "Even though I went through a similar situation, I am sorry. I don't know exactly how you feel." If we are realistic and realize that no one knows exactly what we went through, we don't fall into the self-condemnation of thinking that we did not handle our situation better. What does "better" look like, anyway?

Miscarriages are devastating. Whether you have suffered one or several, each one is difficult. Whether you had a miscarriage before any children were born to you, or you had one in between your other children, it is still equally difficult. You lost a precious, valuable life. Allow this chapter to speak to you wherever it applies, and allow the Holy Spirit to bring peace to your soul. I won't expand on the emotions; you know them. Please also see the healing guidelines in the "Walking Out Your Deliverance" section at the end of this chapter, especially if you have not yet named your child. I am truly sorry for your loss. I, too, have been there.

Grieving an Abortion

Abortion leaves in its wake wounds for a lifetime. I have met women from ages twenty to seventy who have had abortions. It does not matter if they had the abortion two years ago or forty years ago, they still needed healing.

When ministering to women, I ask, "What is holding you back from the fullness of God?"

For many, the answer is always the same: "the abortion I had."

Could you take a moment to think about what is holding you back from the fullness of God? This simple question always leads me to the root of someone's deliverance. Is what's holding you back your paranoia, sexual abuse or feelings of guilt and regret? If you can discover what plagues your mind and consumes your thoughts, you can discover the most important thing you need deliverance from. If you can set your mind free from being tormented with this thing, you will be better able to receive the remainder of your deliverance and instruction from the Lord.

In the case of these women who have had abortions, the loss torments them years later, and some of them still think about the guilt, shame and regret daily. They want to turn the clock back on time and undo what they have done or were forced to do, but they cannot. Teenagers and young adults especially continue suffering long-term emotional aftereffects that surround an abortion. It is not only the loss of the child they aborted that they suffer from; they also suffer from the broken relationships and emotional distress in other areas of their lives that the loss leads to later.

Whether they made the decision in adolescence and in the innocence of not truly knowing what they were doing, or whether they made a purposeful decision, many of these women now live their life for the Lord and know what they did was wrong. They also want their child back. Even though they have other children, these later children don't replace the one(s) these women aborted. These mothers are scarred emotionally until they are led through the healing process.

The continued brokenness of such women (and possibly men, remember) can manifest in a variety of ways. When we feel broken, we can feel depressed and in turmoil emotionally. We can also take our emotions out in unhealthy behaviors and addictions. Here are several ways brokenness can manifest:

- broken relationship with a mother
- a victim mentality
- being overbearing in helping raise a friend's or relative's child
- crying and tearfulness
- being emotionally imbalanced
- having childlike tendencies, not acting age appropriately
- being sexually active in an attempt to fill the void
- feeling prolonged sadness
- food, drug, alcohol and tattoo addictions
- having unprotected sex, hoping to get pregnant again

Forgiveness for Abortion

Many women have been forced to undergo abortions due to pressure from loved ones or parents. Forced abortions could stem from parents supposedly knowing what's best for their unexpectedly pregnant daughter, or thinking their child is too young to carry a child. They might also be worried over their own social status, or that the baby will be unhealthy. Situations in which a woman has had an abortion under duress like that require an additional step in the healing process. The woman needs to extend forgiveness to the person or people who forced the abortion. Bitterness and resentment need to be removed and rooted out. All offense against the offender(s) needs to be abolished. The woman must give up the right to have the person or people pay her back for something she feels she is owed. (This may also be true of a man who did not want a child he had fathered to be aborted, but it happened anyway.) The only way ever to receive that payment is to allow Jesus Christ, who took the payment for all sin on the cross, to remove the hurt, pain, regret and offense.

Women will especially beat themselves up emotionally if they feel as if an abortion was self-induced. Self-induced abortion occurs when a woman drinks or take drugs, and she either purposefully or accidentally ends the baby's life as a result. If this has happened with you, know that although you may have made a mistake, Jesus forgives you when you repent. In the Bible, God tells you, "I have blotted out, like a thick cloud, your transgressions, and like a cloud, your sins. Return to Me, for I have redeemed you" (Isaiah 44:22), and "As far as the east is from the west, so far has He removed our transgressions from us" (Psalm 103:12).

Some women have used the "morning after" pill to shed an unwanted fertilized egg. The pill alters the uterine lining, which prevents the implantation of a fertilized egg into the uterine wall. It assists in thinning the uterine lining, which would need to thicken for an egg to be properly implanted. Since a fertilized egg cannot implant, it is then expelled without the surgical procedure of an abortion. The side effects for the woman taking the pill are nausea, headaches and abdominal pain as the pregnancy terminates.

Women usually take these pills consciously realizing the results. But some have even taken them unaware of the effects. I have ministered to women who had no clue they were aborting a child by taking a pill. They had been falsely informed that the pill would not abort an egg that had already been fertilized, and in their innocence, they believed it.

Years later, when they come into a healing session, one of the first questions they ask is, "I've always wondered, did I abort my child?" The Lord won't make us relive such experiences, but He will bring to the forefront of our mind things we have been unsure about. He does this to bring us to a place of healing. Don't be afraid of what the Holy Spirit wants to reveal. If He leads you to it, He will lead you through it.

Testimonial Letter

After receiving deliverance, a client friend of mine wrote her unborn daughter the following letter:

> Today is the day I found out about you, the day I found out that I was brokenhearted for you. Something I never even knew that I was brokenhearted over, nor did I even really know that you existed. As soon as Kathy started digging and asking questions regarding "that day," I instantly started to cry, and then some of the pieces just started coming together. Things that have been happening in my life throughout the years and in the last few weeks now all make sense, and all the pieces fit together.
>
> Kathy then showed me that you did exist and that you needed a name, and I immediately knew your name. A few weeks ago I looked at my little girl Marinda and thought, *Wow, she is so beautiful,* and then another thought came into my head and I wondered what you looked like. I quickly dismissed this thinking. Why would I think of that? Then maybe last week, I was thinking about your name, writing it down and thinking about how I wanted a "Kaitlin" in this world. Only to know that I did have a Kaitlin. You are absolutely beautiful!!!
>
> There are so many things I wish I would have known. I know you realize that I was young and did not even know that, by taking those two pills, it would then cause your life to take a different turn than what God wanted and what I wanted for you. I am sorry that I don't get to hold you and show you life in this world. Today God gave me a special gift. He let me see you. You were with Jesus, holding His hand, looking at me, smiling and waving, and you are absolutely beautiful. You told me that you are proud of me. And to hear you say that is beyond words or explanation. I want you to know that I love you so much! I just keep replaying that moment of seeing you. I just want to hold onto that and never forget that, not ever. Today is the day I found out about you, and I know today won't be the last.

If you, like my friend, made a bad decision that ended up taking a life through an abortion, write a letter to your child if you think it would help you through the grieving process.

Walking Out Your Deliverance

In the inner healing process of grieving over the loss of a child, there are some specific steps you can take and some guidelines to follow to work through it, depending on your situation. An important first step helpful for a grieving parent is to name your unborn child. If you know the gender, name him or her appropriately. If you don't know the gender, you can pray and ask the Holy Spirit to reveal the gender to you, or you can give your child a gender-neutral name. You can use a name you have always liked, or you can ask the Holy Spirit to reveal a name.

Scriptures on Joy

Psalm 40:1–3; 42:1; Isaiah 61:3; Philippians 4:8

Prayers of Repentance and Forgiveness

Pray this prayer audibly to repent and release forgiveness for abortion:

Heavenly Father, please forgive me for the wrong decisions I have made. I know You created life and that I have no right to choose to take a life. I repent for ending the life of my unborn child(ren).

Lord Jesus, I thank You that You died on the cross to take away my inadequacies. Jesus, I release this child to You. I ask You to forgive me for ending this precious life prematurely. Jesus, I call on You to come heal my heart and take away my pain. Lord, take away the guilt, shame and regret. I now know that what I did was wrong. I choose to move on today and forgive myself.

I do forgive myself. I break agreement with every wrong decision I have made regarding this unborn child, and I release myself from the pain and agony this situation has caused me. I choose today to receive the love of the Father

and the forgiveness of Jesus. I renew my mind to think posi-
tively, so that I will no longer live in the shame of my past.
Thank You, Jesus, for forgiving me, and I forgive myself,
in Your name. Amen.

Pray this prayer audibly to repent and release forgiveness for miscarriage:

Father God, please forgive me for any responsibility I had
in the premature death of my baby. I repent if in any way
my actions, words, care of my body or trauma led to my
miscarriage.
I receive Your forgiveness, Jesus, and I also forgive myself.
I forgive myself for the part I feel I had in ending this life
before birth. I forgive myself and receive the finished, ac-
complished work of the cross, through which I am forgiven,
in Your name. Amen.

Next, please seek the Holy Spirit regarding other people you need to forgive who were attached to the situation surrounding the loss of your unborn child (whether through abortion or miscarriage). Individually speak out the names of each person, if you know those names. Ask the Lord to forgive you for the feelings you have harbored against any of them. Forgive them and spend time in your soul making peace with them and with the situation. Some of these people may include:

- A sexual partner for being involved with you in the sex act
- An offender who sexually abused you
- Parents or other adults for not stopping known sexual abuse against you
- Parents or a sexual partner for forcing you to have an abortion
- Relatives for incest and molestation of you

- Doctors, medical professionals, abortion clinics and staff who were involved in your medical appointments and procedures
- The person who caused an accident or trauma that resulted in your miscarriage

When you have identified the people involved, pray this prayer audibly to repent yourself and release forgiveness of them:

Father, I choose to break agreement with unforgiveness and with the sense of entitlement that I am owed something in the natural or spiritual realm because of these people who have hurt or abused me and who have contributed to the death of my baby. I choose to release each offender of his or her offense.

Lord, I also release the feelings, emotions and demonic strongholds of hate, rage, anger, offense, bitterness, resentment, guilt, condemnation, regret and the shame of losing a child. Rampant feelings and emotions running wild and controlling me, I command you to stop now, in Jesus' name!

Jesus, I say that I choose to move forward with confidence, hope and peace, leaning and relying on You, the Author and Finisher of our life and faith, in Your name. Amen.

When it comes to the loss of an unborn child, besides releasing forgiveness to others, you also may need to seek forgiveness both from others and from yourself. If necessary and you have not already done so, and if you feel convicted by the Holy Spirit about this, ask forgiveness from the child's other parent if you made a decision or acted without his or her permission. Also if necessary and if you feel led to do so, go and discuss the situation—and healing from it—with anyone else who was involved who may also be suffering from remorse over decisions they made. An example would be to talk to your parents and tell them you forgive them if they forced you into a decision that ended your child's life. This will bring healing to their soul as well as yours.

Often, the most difficult thing we can do is forgive ourselves. We want to hold ourselves in captivity and punish ourselves by staying in emotional pain. This is not the Lord's intention for us. He bore our shame and pain. Forgiving yourself may take repeated attempts, but I suggest you start by praying out loud this simple statement: *Lord, I forgive myself.* Pray this out loud as many times as you need to. You may have to come back to it and try it again another day. You may forgive yourself today and then take in the feelings again tomorrow. It is okay; just get up tomorrow and speak it out again. Declare it and find peace in saying to yourself, *I can do this. It will be all right. I am forgiven!*

Spirits to Discern and Cast Out

Ask the Holy Spirit to reveal all the demonic spirits associated with grief and loss (whether the loss of a child or some different loss) that you need to cast out. Out loud, command these spirits to leave: "Spirit of _____, go, in Jesus' name!" You may have to do this several times over a period of time. Do it until you feel peace, a release or a spiritual shift. Spirits often associated with grief and loss:

Abortion, condemnation, death, guilt, hate, insecurity, murder, regret, resentment, self-hate, shame, unworthiness

Prayer of Activation

Heavenly Father, fill me with Your love and peace. Give me hope where I've felt hopeless.
Holy Spirit, I draw on You to be my comforter and friend.

Declarations to Speak Out

Speak out the following faith declarations and spiritual warfare declarations that are specific to the loss of a child. Bookmark these pages and come back to them as often as necessary to assist you in renewing your mind, transforming your heart and increasing your faith.

Faith Declarations for Grief Associated with the Loss of a Child

Make these faith declarations audibly, with power and authority, believing that you will receive them. Speak them out from a position of *I have these*, not *I'm trying to obtain these*. While you transition from the grief of losing a child into healing and peace, read these declarations out regularly to help you grow strong in faith and renew your mind.

- I declare that I am free in Christ!
- I speak life into my body, my emotions and my soul. I will not be held in a spirit of captivity any longer.
- I order all demonic assignments of guilt and shame to be abolished and incinerated from my life. I will go forth in the strength of the Lord.
- I rebuke the devourer and all attempts to use this situation to steal, kill and destroy any future children from coming forth, in Jesus' name.
- I reverse any side effects of abortions or miscarriages on my body. Spirits of death coming against my children, I say be gone, in Jesus' name!
- I speak and declare that no weapon formed against my generational line and producing life will prosper.
- I believe that I have received the freedom Christ came to offer me.
- I decree and declare that I have forgiven myself for past mistakes and that I will walk in that forgiveness.
- Jesus came to give us abundant life, and I receive it!
- I receive freedom in my thoughts from guilt, condemnation, regret and shame, in Jesus' name.

Spiritual Warfare Declarations for Grief Associated with the Loss of a Child

Make these spiritual warfare declarations audibly, with power and authority. When you speak out these declarations, you are taking up your God-given authority to bind and restrict the enemy and counteract future attacks. Declare them repeatedly, until you feel something release in the spiritual atmosphere.

- Devil, for everything you have stolen, killed and destroyed in my life, I command the blessings of the Lord to come back upon me.
- I rebuke and renounce spirits of death, in Jesus' name.
- I declare that I am an overcomer, and that I am victorious. I order all assignments against my victory to be aborted, in Jesus' name.
- I remove any hindrance and barrier I have constructed in the spiritual realm as a result of my actions.
- I speak and declare that I am made in the image of God. I am loved and cherished by Him and am therefore not condemned. There is no condemnation for those in Christ Jesus.
- Enemy, I speak to you, and I call off your assignment on my children and family line. You will not have them! Their destiny is marked for the Kingdom of God.
- I remove every spirit of destruction hindering my future, in Jesus' name.
- I rebuke the devourer and tell him to abort his assignment and mission against me, in Jesus' name!

CHAPTER 12

ADDICTIONS

Self-Assessment Test—Spirit of Addiction

On a scale of 1 to 10, rate each statement below.

1. I feel the need to escape from things and situations.
2. I don't have a healthy outlet in which to relieve stress.
3. When I get angry, I react in the flesh instead of running to God.
4. I try to control my life with what I do, because my life seems so out of control.
5. Food is my friend; I am an emotional eater.
6. I am often tempted by lustful, perverse thoughts.
7. I spend unnecessary amounts of time on electronics because I am bored, even though I really have plenty of other things I could do

I am addicted to Jesus. In different song lyrics and sayings, people will sing or talk about how "I'm addicted to You." In the song Eddie James wrote, "I'm Addicted," the lyrics talk about how he is addicted to Jesus and nothing else will satisfy.

Do you have an addiction? Many people suffer from addictions such as food addiction, substance abuse, TV, electronics, Internet usage, sexual addictions and pornography. Your addiction takes hold because nothing else is satisfying you. As you have received healing and deliverance throughout this book, however, I pray that now, in this final chapter, you will have already found so much freedom that you can finish the process by removing any final addictions as you read these last pages.

As you read through this chapter, note that because each kind of addiction is important to deal with individually, the organization is a little bit different. Immediately after each addiction we discuss, I have included a separate "Walking Out Your Deliverance" section that is specific to being delivered from that particular stronghold. First, I cover food addictions and provide the "Walking Out" section to help you with deliverance from eating issues. Then I talk about substance abuse and provide deliverance helps for those kinds of addictions. Next, I consider electronic and Internet addictions and include deliverance helps for those. Finally, I talk about sexual addictions, with their own "Walking Out" section. One by one, work through the sections that are applicable to you in finding your freedom.

Truly, only Jesus can satisfy. Let's take this final journey together and remove the temporary satisfaction you get from the world and the lusts of the flesh, so you can receive your complete deliverance and find lasting satisfaction in Him.

Food Addictions

Food addicts come in all shapes and sizes—Caucasian and Latino and every other ethnicity, skinny and heavy, homemakers and business professionals, children and adults, and even clergy. Food addiction knows no limits or boundaries. There is a saying, "Food is your friend." I like to say, "Eat to survive, not to thrive." In my book *A Worship-Woven Life* (Tate Publishing, 2014), I dedicated a chapter to how your plate of food is an act of worship. I encourage you to look at what you eat as a plate of worship and seek the Holy Spirit for guidance on what to eat. He alone knows what is best for your body.

I know about food addicts because I have been surrounded by many friends who struggle with food addiction. The Lord has led our ministry to take a stand against food addictions and help people become free of unhealthy eating, turning them toward biblical eating principles.

You may think, *Why are we talking about food addictions in an inner healing and deliverance book?* Because food addictions are rooted in an emotional imbalance that needs to be healed. If you can identify with even one of the types of food addictions I will talk about, and if you go to food for relief from your problems and hurts, you need healing.

Discover what type of addictive food eater you are by spending time with the Holy Spirit and asking Him to reveal your food triggers. Until you receive emotional healing, you will not be able to conquer your food addiction. When the next emotionally intense or negative situation arises, you will discover yourself running to food again. The key to deliverance is discovering the root cause.

Types of Food Addictions

There are many different types of food addictions and many different causes. Among those people addicted to food we find stress eaters, comfort eaters, control eaters, boredom eaters, emotional eaters and unaware eaters. Let's look at what each type looks like and some possible root causes.

Stress eaters

At the first sign of conflict, stress eaters run to food. Their reasoning is that if they eat something, it will take their mind off their stress, relieve it and give them peace. They have not been taught stress management, so they go into turmoil when stress occurs.

Comfort eaters

Comfort eaters eat because it soothes and relaxes them. They may or may not have conflict in their lives, but either way, food is a friend. Eating brings them satisfaction, along with joy and happiness where they might not find those elsewhere. They can be either social people or lonely people; both can become comfort eaters. Eating becomes a hobby for them, but it is still an unhealthy addiction.

Control eaters

Even when you can't control anything else in your life, you can control what you put in your mouth. Control eaters have a food addiction because food is the only thing they can control. If they were controlled by a parent and now are adults, they may have issues from the past that need healing. If their current life is out of control due to unforeseen circumstances, or if they are being controlled by someone else, they will eat because food is the only thing they can control. They eat whatever they want, whenever they want, because it gives them a sense of having control over something.

Boredom eaters

Food is enjoyment to a boredom eater. They eat because it breaks up the monotony in their life and gives them something to do. They are not always bored, but the boredom they do experience can lead to addiction or depression. They have a need that nothing else satisfies except food. They feel stuck, empty, restless and unmotivated. There is an unexplainable unsettledness in them. Eating is an escape, a desire "to do something" less invasive than having to deal with their problems, physical appearance or emotional traumas.

Emotional eaters

Emotional eaters love to graze all day and are munchers. They are always snacking and feel a strong desire to have food in their mouth, in their hands and in their vehicles. Whenever they leave home, they have food in tote. They justify with their words what they are eating and why. They even try to believe it's okay to be eating all the time because they are snacking on healthy food. Still, they continually eat and cannot stop, so it's an addiction. It can vary from a single cookie to a whole bag of potato chips. On the road, they will stop at a gas station to grab a candy bar and pop, or they will hit the drive-thru and grab some fries and sweet tea.

Emotional eaters consistently taste food they are cutting up and cooking. As they prepare it, they are not tasting it simply to test the seasoning; they eat part of it while standing at the counter. They will justify this as simply eating the scraps while cooking and putting food away. They eat just because, and they often cram more food into an already full stomach.

Unaware eaters

Some people are unaware that they even struggle with food addiction. They claim simply to love food. They love the taste and enjoy eating it. They don't sit and pile up a big plate of food, but when they are done and satisfied, they go back for second helpings or another small piece because it tastes so good. They know they have had enough already and will regret second helpings after the food settles in their stomach. They go back for another portion anyway, however, just because they enjoy eating, and they justify it by saying it tastes good.

Eating too much or not knowing when to say "stop, I've had enough" is not a healthy habit; it's a problem. We need to recognize it for what it is, a food addiction. It is not necessarily an emotional food addiction, but it is still a lack of self-control and self-discipline. We should be eating to glorify the name of the Lord. Our plate of food should be our act of worship to Him. Our bodies are temples of the Holy Spirit, and we are called to take care of them.

Move Up and Forward

In order to be free from food addiction, you have to want to be free. You cannot lose weight or give up food for anyone other than yourself. People have tried to lose weight for all the wrong reasons, such as for a loved one or to look better and feel better, but have failed in trying. Changing your eating habits and releasing a food addiction is a matter of the mind. You have to want to change and purpose in your mind to do so. Until you purpose in your heart and mind to do this for yourself, it isn't going to happen.

You cannot break your food addiction or change your size unless you want to do it for yourself. You need to develop deep determination. You have to want it, and then set your mind so that nothing will stand in your way and prevent it. Once you determine in your heart and mind that you want to change, then you will be victorious in your quest.

Changing our eating habits and losing weight requires a lifestyle change. These things are not something we do for a season. They require constant battle and effort, so we have to establish a plan for the rest of our lives. If we ever go back and take on our old ways, then we have lost the battle and will end up fighting it all over again. It is about developing healthy choices, becoming emotionally healthy and changing what we eat for a lifetime. It also requires becoming educated on proper nutrition and good, healthy eating habits. It is about leaving our emotional bondages behind us and walking forward in freedom and victory. I have a saying, "Up and forward," that applies here. You need to move up toward your goals and forward into your destiny, and that comes through seeking deliverance.

You can also pray and command your brain functions surrounding your appetite to become normal. Declare to your body that it will come into alignment with the Word of God. Command the neural center in your brain—the part that regulates your appetite—to function properly. Command your hypothalamus to help regulate food intake. Command your appestat control center, which controls hunger and also regulates food intake, to come into alignment with the Word of God and be normal, in Jesus' name.

Food Disorders and the Demonic

Demonic spirits can also be attached to eating disorders and will need to be cast out. One indication is that people lose weight, and then they seem to gain it back. We need to go deep and cast out any spirits attached to our food disorders. Emotional ailments can lead to these disorders. So although we are responsible for some of our eating habits, demonic strongmen can also be attacking us in the area of our appetite.

When we cast out a demonic spirit associated with our emotional ailment and food disorder, we will discover that walking in freedom from food addiction gets easier. Deliverance will minimize the temptation because we have received inner healing, but we still have our own part to play in being delivered of this stronghold. We still need to exhibit self-control and discipline ourselves in our eating habits.

I like 1 Corinthians 9:27, a verse that has spoken to me in many ways: "But I discipline my body and bring it into subjection, lest, when I have preached to others, I myself should become disqualified." I believe that as ministers in Christ and as Christians living to share the Gospel, we should hear this verse speaking volumes to us. How can we be witnesses and living testimonies to others if we are overweight? As I preach of the healing atonement of Jesus Christ, I don't want my body to disqualify the Gospel for my hearers. I believe we need to be a testimony of what Christ can do in us and for us in the areas of weight loss and healthy eating.

As Christians, we need to get rid of our food addictions, emotional bondages and excess weight so we can be effective for the Kingdom. How can we preach healing and deliverance if we are held in bondage to food? How will people listen to us and value what we say? We need to make the Gospel of Christ credible through our own testimony. How can we have healing lines and major crusades where we are praying for people if we cannot stand on our feet for ten hours because we have too much weight on our bodies?

We need to get moving as the Body of Christ and be a testimony of Christ's goodness and freedom. If we want to set the captives free, then that freedom has to start with us. We need to get rid of the emotional baggage that makes us go to food instead of to the Word of God. We need to dive in deep and digest what the Word says instead of digesting more food. We need to know what God says about us instead of turning to the temporary gratification food can give us. We need to get right so we can fight the good fight and bring others to the saving knowledge of Christ Jesus.

Addictive eating is triggered by a root problem. You need to find the root problem that is causing you to eat, and then you need to receive deliverance. It is only through the process of deliverance, self-control and determination that you will be able to uproot and destroy your food addiction.

Walking Out Your Deliverance

As you receive emotional healing from your food addiction, be aware that there are natural remedies that can also assist in weight loss and help ward off food cravings. You can curb sugar addictions by taking magnesium supplements, eating more protein and retraining your pallet with natural sugars such as raw honey, pure maple syrup, coconut sugar or monk fruit sugar. Using raw cocoa powder also helps. Drinking more water assists in weight loss, too, along with drinking green tea and using apple cider vinegar.

Scriptures about Relying on God

Psalm 5:3; 9:9; 18:2; 37:5; 62:7; 121:2; Isaiah 26:4; 41:13

Prayer of Repentance and Forgiveness

Pray this prayer audibly to repent and release forgiveness:

Heavenly Father, forgive me for thinking less of myself and not valuing myself. Help me see myself as You do. Thank You, Father, that You made me in Your image, perfect and complete. I can see now that You love me, and that food does not define me. I choose to forgive everyone who has spoken negative words over my life that made me run to food for comfort and satisfaction. I know that truly, only You can satisfy and fill the void in my life. I trust in You completely to help me walk out of my food addictions and conquer them by faith, in Jesus' name. Amen.

Spirits to Discern and Cast Out

Ask the Holy Spirit to reveal all the demonic spirits associated with food addictions that you need to cast out. Out loud, command these spirits to leave: "Spirit of _____, go, in Jesus' name!" You may have to do this several times over a period of time. Do it until you feel peace, a release or a spiritual shift. Spirits often associated with food addictions:

Anorexia, bondage to food, bulimia, caffeine addiction, chocolate addiction, complacency, deep hurt, depression, despair, discouragement, disobedience, failure, food addiction, gluttony, idolatry, laziness, loneliness, lust, lust of the eyes, lust of the flesh, obesity, overeating, passivity, pride, purging, rejection, self-indulgence, stress, sugar addiction, suicide, ungodly appetites, unworthiness

Prayer of Activation

Father God, fill me with Your love. When I am weak, make me strong. Help me see myself as You do: beloved, chosen and beautiful. I receive Your love. I open my heart and mind to be deeply connected with You. I receive everything You want to teach me. Instruct me this day.

Holy Spirit, I receive Your conviction about the food I eat and when and how much I eat.

I thank You, Father, that I am blessed, and I receive Your blessings and comfort, in Jesus' name. Amen.

Declarations to Speak Out

Speak out the following faith declarations and spiritual warfare declarations. Bookmark these pages and come back to them as often as necessary to assist you in renewing your mind, transforming your heart and increasing your faith.

Faith Declarations

Make these faith declarations audibly, with power and authority, believing that you will receive them. Speak them out from a position of *I have these*, not *I'm trying to obtain these*. While you transition from food addictions to freedom and healthy eating habits, read these declarations out regularly to help you grow strong in faith and renew your mind.

- I declare that I am free from food bondages and that I make wise choices in my eating.

- I proclaim liberation in my emotions. I speak and decree that my emotions are stable and well-balanced, and that they align with God's Word.
- I command my appestat control center to come into alignment with the Word of God.
- I decree that I will not overeat, but will stop when I am satisfied.
- I speak and decree that food is not my comfort, because the Holy Spirit is my Comforter!
- I proclaim that my body is a temple of the Holy Spirit, and I will eat to glorify His temple.
- I say that my plate of food is an act of worship, and when I sit down to eat, I will eat to honor Jesus' name.
- I proclaim that I am healthy, fit and ready to advance the Kingdom, in Jesus' name.

Spiritual Warfare Declarations

Make these spiritual warfare declarations audibly, with power and authority. When you speak out these declarations, you are taking up your God-given authority to bind and restrict the enemy and counteract future attacks. Declare them repeatedly, until you feel something release in the spiritual atmosphere.

- I command every assignment of the devil trying to steal my destiny through unhealthy eating habits, obesity and food addictions to leave now, in Jesus' name.
- I command every spirit of abortion and every destiny destroyer spirit coming against my life to leave, in Jesus' name. You will not abort and destroy the assignment God has for my life!
- I command every demonic spirit infiltrating my thoughts and drawing me to stress eating, or to comfort, control, boredom, emotional or unaware eating, to leave my soul now, in Jesus' name.

- Every demon penetrating my soul and creating a seducing spirit to draw me into unhealthy and unproductive eating, I call off your assignment over my life, in Jesus' name!
- Every generational curse of food addiction, depression, high blood pressure, high cholesterol, heart disease and obesity, I break agreement with you, and I command you to release me now, in Jesus' name. Get out and stay out!
- Every demonic assignment attempting to penetrate my thoughts with unworthiness, insecurity, fear and uncleanliness, I call off your assignment now, in the name of Yahweh!
- I believe and receive the freedom Christ purchased for me at the cross, and I state and claim that I live in victory and freedom from food addictions, in Jesus' name.

Smoking, Drinking and Substance Abuse

Addictions are tough to break, but through Christ, anything and everything is possible. You can do it! The question is, Will you do it? You have to want to change and want to be released of these crutches in your life. Receiving deliverance from substance abuse addictions requires self-discipline, inner healing, casting out the associated demons and making lifestyle changes. The spirits leave immediately when cast out, but our learning to resist temptation and change bad habits may take more time and effort. I know this can happen instantly, but it is usually not the norm. You have to desire to change, repent, forgive yourself and be ready to move forward despite opposition. Realize that you are a new person in Christ, and that through the strength of the Holy Spirit you have the power to leave bad habits and cravings for unhealthy substances behind.

I believe the best prayer we can pray is, "Holy Spirit, convict me and take away my desire for these things." We need to allow the Holy Spirit to work on our heart to bring change. He has given us a free will, and it is our will, mind and emotions that keep us in bondage to feeling false satisfaction from these substances.

The casting out of spirits attached to addictive habits is very important. People who suffer substance addiction often can stop smoking or drinking for a period of years. All of a sudden, however, when they go through a tragic event the first thing they go back to is their former addiction. The problem is that they never had the demonic spirits or influences attached to their addictions cast out. The demonic spirits of smoking, alcoholism and substance abuse went dormant and slumbering inside them. The spirits were inactive, but then they activated when sin or stress in these people's lives manifested. How the people reacted to challenge or trauma activated the once-dormant spirits.

If such spirits were never cast out, they lie slumbering inside, and when something terrible happens to a person, they reactivate and the person finds himself or herself rediscovering the same negative pattern as before. The person may have been genuinely walking out his or her freedom for years, but then he or she slipped back into the old ways because demons associated with the addiction were not cast out. That is why people can go back to substance abuse after being free even five years or more. It is so important to go deep down to the roots and pull out every demonic manifestation that could hinder us today or in the future.

When you are drinking, smoking and taking drugs, you are masking a problem. You are trying to achieve a high or bring your mind into a relaxed state so you don't have to think about your problems and you can mask them with a temporary fix. The challenge is that the fix is only temporary. Deliverance is permanent and complete. The attacks don't have to come back.

Relieving ourselves from bondage to substance abuse includes receiving the love of the Father in His fullness. Seek Him to find your comfort and solace. Build a strong relationship with Jesus, which is also key. Depend and rely on Him, not on a substance, to satisfy. Trust Him in any experience you face that you feel you cannot handle, and trust Him for your future.

Walking Out Your Deliverance

As I have said, emotional ailments are often related to spiritual strongholds. When we suffer from unhealthy or negative emotions and don't seek our healing, these emotions can build up and create in us a demonic spiritual stronghold. If your substance abuse is highly triggered by something emotional that you feel you can no longer control in the natural, then take time now to stop and pray, and consider whether or not there is a demonic entity at work in your emotions that is leading you into substance abuse addiction.

Scriptures on Strength

Psalm 11:19; 28:7–8; 46:1–3; Proverbs 18:10; Isaiah 40:29, 31; 2 Corinthians 12:9–10; Philippians 4:13

Prayer of Repentance and Forgiveness

Pray this prayer audibly to repent and release forgiveness:

Heavenly Father, I ask Your forgiveness for abusing my body, which is Your temple, through smoking, drugs and/ or alcohol. I repent for the past and thank You, Lord, that I have changed my ways and have walked out of unhealthy behavioral patterns, habits and addictions. Today, I make a commitment to You never to go back into these habits.

I command all slumbering and dormant spirits to arise and vacate my body, in the mighty name of Jesus. I command that there will be no more addictive spirits in my body, the temple of the Holy Spirit. I command all spirits of tar, nicotine, smoking, chewing, drug addictions, alcoholism, hallucinogens, drinking and generational curses of abusive substances to leave, in Jesus' name. I claim, command and decree that my body is free from these demonic influences, which are never to return.

I ask You, Lord, to seal the good work You have done in me now, and to cover me in the blood of Christ. In the name of Jesus, I pray.

Spirits to Discern and Cast Out

Ask the Holy Spirit to reveal all the demonic spirits associated with substance addictions that you need to cast out. Out loud, command these spirits to leave: "Spirit of _____, go, in Jesus' name!" You may have to do this several times over a period of time. Do it until you feel peace, a release or a spiritual shift. Spirits often associated with substance abuse:

Addiction, alcoholism, chewing, drinking, generational spirits, hallucinogens, nicotine, smoking, tar

Prayer of Activation

Heavenly Father, I receive Your love for me. I thank You that Your Son, Jesus, died for me. I release my need for addictive substances, and I receive Your Holy Spirit in all His fullness. I speak and decree that every side effect from substance abuse has left me. I thank You that I rely and depend on Your Son, Jesus, to be my peace and strength. I receive Your shalom now. I believe You have every good and perfect thing waiting for me. I receive my emotional and physical healing, and all that Your Son, Jesus, purchased for me. I activate my faith to believe for the best possible life, living in the fullness and completeness of Christ, in Jesus' name. Amen.

Declarations to Speak Out

Speak out the following faith declarations and spiritual warfare declarations. Bookmark these pages and come back to them as often as necessary to assist you in renewing your mind, transforming your heart and increasing your faith.

Faith Declarations

Make these faith declarations audibly, with power and author-ity, believing that you will receive them. Speak them out from a position of *I have these*, not *I'm trying to obtain these*. While you transition from substance addictions to freedom and dependence on Christ instead, read these declarations out regularly to help you grow strong in faith and renew your mind.

- I declare that I will put my trust in God instead of in a substance to satisfy me.
- I proclaim that I do not need to depend on a substance to find joy and to release stress.
- I call forth a greater faith, and when I am tempted, I will draw on that faith to lead me through my temptations.
- I speak and declare that I am free from cravings, seduc-ing spirits and the draw to find comfort in a temporary fix or satisfaction, instead of in God, who is everlasting satisfaction.
- I will trust in You, Lord, for all the situations and circum-stances I face, and I will rely on the Holy Spirit within me to get me through.
- I rely on my most dependable God to satisfy me at all time.
- I take dominion and authority over every temptation that comes my way, and I declare that I have the strength of the Lord to resist temptation, in Jesus' name.

Spiritual Warfare Declarations

Make these spiritual warfare declarations audibly, with power and authority. When you speak out these declarations, you are taking up your God-given authority to bind and restrict the enemy and counteract future attacks. Declare them repeatedly, until you feel something release in the spiritual atmosphere.

- I decree and declare that every seducing, luring spirit will get out of me, in Jesus' name.
- I bind and restrict every spirit operating over me and through me that is trying to keep me in bondage to substance abuse.
- I command all demonic attachments, defilements and transferences from the abuse of any substances to be removed from my body and cast out, in Jesus' name.
- I command and call off every generational spirit related to my addiction. I speak and decree that I will not fall into the same generational curses as my ancestors.
- I break off and call off any and all of the effects of my addictions from also affecting my children. I decree that generational curses going forward are now broken, in Jesus' name.
- I annihilate every principality operating against me to keep me in bondage.
- I speak and decree that the emotional baggage that once infiltrated my soul is gone now, in Jesus' name, and I therefore do not need to depend on abusing substances.
- I bind and restrict every demonic operation against me and release it of its assignment, in Jesus' name.

Electronic Addictions

Electronic addictions can include addictions to items such as the TV, computers, video games and cell phones. We live in a day and age of advanced technology, and while I am thrilled with this technology that allows me to share the message of Jesus worldwide, we have to be careful. Let's look at a few of these electronic addictions.

Phone addictions

Talking or texting on our cell phone can be addictive. This can be a challenge for businesspeople and ministry workers who need to be available to their clients and the people who inquire about their services. I used to disrupt our family dinners, thinking, *What if someone on the other end of the phone is suicidal?* People want us to be at their beck and call, and in this day and age of texting, we no longer have days off or nights off. People expect us to be on 24/7.

The phone has ruined marriages and implanted rejection into the actual person in the room who is feeling ignored and left out. We are often forgetful of the people right in front of us who crave our attention. People have even turned their bathrooms into offices so they can use the extra moments on the toilet or in the bathtub to conduct business or chat away. We have gotten to the point that we can't put our phones down in a restaurant or at the dinner table. Even if we happen to have company with us in the living room, we lay our phone next to us screen side up so we can glance at whoever is calling or texting.

When not talking on the phone, we use it to scroll through our social media newsfeeds, check our emails and send text messages. Then, even though we just did it, we cycle through the same pattern all over again. What started as a quick ten-minute check has now consumed forty minutes of our time. We act as if we are bored and have nothing else to do, so we get on our phone. Addicted to social media and Internet searching, we are on our phone almost constantly. At the root of this is a luring and/or boredom spirit.

Gaming addictions

Video game addiction, whether on a TV screen, a computer or a cell phone, is a serious problem. There are people who would rather be playing a game than spending time with their family. Gaming addictions can develop through playing any game out there, but particularly through demonic games such as *Dungeons and Dragons*, *World of Warcraft*, *Ruins of Magic* or *Everquest*. Adult men have made these games their "job and family." They would rather play these games than go out and work to support their family. They make their wife work, or they do all they can to qualify for unemployment income so they have more time for gaming. The games they play are intense and addictive and require all their attention. They would rather not get off the computer at all, playing as long as they can, until they must sleep.

I know of a man who literally sat and played a video game continually for a few years straight and ignored his family. He was so addicted that if they asked him a question, he would yell at them because they were interrupting him. This family never ate dinner at the table together, and he did not help with the kids, run errands or work. His children basically did not have a father, and they ended up with severe rejection issues and emotional problems.

These games are demonically influenced spiritual warfare, and people need deliverance from them. Such games ruin family units and cause divorce and dissension, making family members feel abandoned and rejected.

TV addictions

You can also be addicted to the TV, computer or other electronics without it being demonic. People have a tendency to use electronics as a friend or companion, or as a tool for gossip and other things that are unproductive. People come home from work and turn on the TV to relax and unwind. They sit down to watch the news, and soon after, they discover they got hooked on one show after another and ended up wasting their entire evening in front of the TV.

Electronic addictions make people stay up late, compromise their sleep and yell at their family if someone talks during a show or walks in front of the TV. These addictions deteriorate family relationships. Elderly and disabled people also become addicted to TV due to loneliness and lack of purpose. They often sit around just waiting for life to end. Yet I think such people could become our greatest intercessors and could be valuable for the Kingdom of God. Everyone has a purpose, and when these people have nothing else, they have God, and they can pray.

Kingdom mindedness

Kingdom mindedness should be our priority. What are we doing that is productive and fruitful to advance the Kingdom of God? Our relationship with the Lord should be our first priority. Our life has purpose, and we need to complete that purpose our Lord has given us. We need to set goals. We need to be Kingdom minded instead of worldly minded.

Pray and ask the Holy Spirit to convict you about your TV show watching and what you allow in your eye gates and ear gates. Expect Him to stir a desire in you to want to do more than passively sit around watching TV. Electronics can distract us from our time with the Lord. People will justify their electronic addiction by saying they are getting sermons and prophetic insights from YouTube, social media and the Internet. We need to go to our Father God first and our Bible, however, and get our own inspired lesson from the Holy Spirit before we seek it on the Internet. Our relationship with the Trinity should be our priority, and what we get through media sources is just an added blessing.

Electronic addictions have a way of stealing our time. When we are caught up in a show and are tired at the end of a long day, we would rather veg out and relax than study our Bible or go to prayer. We make excuses such as that we have to chill or take a nap, and then time slips by and we have left Adonai out of another day.

One way to set yourself free from electronic addictions is to find a hobby. Find something else that brings you joy, helps you unwind and is relaxing. Start actively communicating with your spouse and children. Find out what makes them want to spend so much time with electronics, and assist them on their way to finding freedom. Don't settle for addictive behavior in your family or yourself, and don't settle for less than God's best in your marriage. Don't think your spouse can't or won't change. With Christ at the center, everything is possible for those who believe.

You need to raise your expectations! If you want to change, it starts with intercession. Make some declarations to break off these strongholds and addictive spirits (for example, see the declarations in the section that follows). Christ came to set the captives free. Let the captives be set free today, in Jesus' name!

Walking Out Your Deliverance

If you want to break electronic addictions, you have to take an active part in doing so. Give your family suggestions about how to break their addictive electronic habits, too, and have a discussion with your spouse if this is a problem in your home. Find family activities such as playing games, going to a park or walking around the mall to get you active and busy. Boredom can be the driving force behind electronic addictions. Remove inactivity by being active in your walk with the Lord through prayer and Bible study.

Scriptures on Knowing God

Deuteronomy 30:14; Psalm 34:8; Isaiah 55:6; Jeremiah 33:3; John 4:24; 15:5; Romans 5:8; Hebrews 11:6

Prayer of Repentance and Forgiveness

Pray this prayer audibly to repent and release forgiveness:

Father God, please forgive me for being addicted to electronics. I know Your Word says we must have no other gods and idols before You. I am sorry for making electronics an idol and a god in my life. I speak and declare that this day, I choose to change my behaviors. I will not participate in unhealthy ways of seeking satisfaction from worldly things. I know only You can satisfy, and I will commit myself to spending more time with You.

I forgive myself for not recognizing my electronic addiction sooner and for being lazy and slothful in breaking my addiction to these things. Please convict me, Holy Spirit, when I turn to electronics and have not spent ample time with You. I release these things and the importance they have in my life to You. I declare that I am changed, and I break the necessity for these things in my life, in Jesus' name. Amen!

Spirits to Discern and Cast Out

Ask the Holy Spirit to reveal all the demonic spirits associated with electronic addictions that you need to cast out. Out loud, command these spirits to leave: "Spirit of _____, go, in Jesus' name!" You may have to do this several times over a period of time. Do it until you feel peace, a release or a spiritual shift. Spirits often associated with electronic addictions:

Addiction, boredom, electronics, false companionship, generational curses, loneliness, rebellion

Prayer of Activation

I prophesy a miracle of freedom to come into my home and my life! I claim, command and decree that the bondage of electronic addiction be no more. I command all strongholds to be broken, and freedom to come! I command and call forth unity and oneness in my marriage and my family unit. I say that we are a family who enjoys spending time together and conversing. I call forth my desire to spend time with the Lord through prayer, praise and the Word. I speak out that I have energy and strength, and that I love to be active in my faith. I declare that I put fruitful and productive things into my soul that can benefit the Kingdom. I thank You, Father, for this breakthrough, in Jesus' name. Amen!

Declarations to Speak Out

Speak out the following faith declarations and spiritual warfare declarations. Bookmark these pages and come back to them as often as necessary to assist you in renewing your mind, transforming your heart and increasing your faith.

Faith Declarations

Make these faith declarations audibly, with power and authority, believing that you will receive them. Speak them out from a position of *I have these*, not *I'm trying to obtain these*. While you transition from electronic addictions to productivity for the Kingdom, read these declarations out regularly to help you grow strong in faith and renew your mind.

- I come against any and all seducing and luring spirits that would draw me to electronics, and I *break* them, in Jesus' name.
- I come against any false idol in my life, anything that would draw me to it more than to God, and I say be removed, in Jesus' name. Be removed and destroyed now, by the blood of the Lamb!
- I command all unctions from within that are not from the Spirit of the Lord to be cast down and out from within, in Jesus' name.
- I paralyze the powers of darkness that would draw me in an unhealthy way, including drawing me into social media addictions, TV and electronic game addictions, movie addictions and anything that takes my eyes off of God.
- Father, forgive me and this technology generation for the ease of turning to electronics instead of You.
- Forgive me for setting anything above You or before You.
- I break agreement with the necessity of these items in my life and the attention I give them, in Jesus' name.

236

Spiritual Warfare Declarations

Make these spiritual warfare declarations audibly, with power and authority. When you speak out these declarations, you are taking up your God-given authority to bind and restrict the enemy and counteract future attacks. Declare them repeatedly, until you feel something release in the spiritual atmosphere.

- I rebuke, annihilate and dismantle all powers of the airwaves coming against me, my family and the world to draw us into media addictions.
- Every false, lying spirit of electronics and media, I command you to break your hold on me, in Jesus' name. Break your hold now!
- Every prince and power of the air, relent of your assignment now; you are disintegrated by the blood of the Lamb.
- Every evil deploy sent to attack the airwaves and the Internet, I say be relinquished of your assignment, in Jesus' name. You will abort your mission and fail, in Jesus' name.
- Every monitoring spirit reporting back to commanders, I render you blind, deaf and mute, in Jesus' name. You will not monitor through the airwaves.
- I command all demonic frequency and communication channels to be blocked and stopped up, in Jesus' name.
- Enemy, I rebuke you and your influences over this generation, me and my family. I deploy angels to activate on behalf of the Kingdom of God.
- Every demonic marker written and traced through electronics and frequencies, I vanish your reports with the fire of God. Be removed of your assignment, in Jesus' name.
- Every spirit operating against me because of my past addiction, I eradicate you and your mission, in Jesus' name.

Sexual Addictions

Sexual sin brings with it self-condemnation, regret, shame, guilt and embarrassment. It has entry doors and points that can be established throughout our lives. The root causes of sexual sin can vary, but they all need to be discovered and dealt with for people to find freedom.

Perversion

The root cause of sexual sin could be something you were exposed to, an experience you went through, a defilement that happened to you or a door to sin and perversion that you opened. Sexual sin is not a man's disease; it is everyone's disease. While people may identify perversion as an illness, it is actually rooted in strong demonic activity.

There are people in sexual sin who think they are safe in it. They think that as long as no one knows what they are doing, they are okay. Unfortunately, they are not safe. Whether they are involved in pornography, masturbation or adultery, they are in captivity.

Often, sexual sin becomes an addictive behavioral pattern where emotions of unworthiness set in and people begin an internal, emotional spiral downward. On the outside, their appearance and emotions seem fine, but inside, they cannot forget the captivity they are experiencing. Daily these thoughts consume their mind, and they are desperate to reach out and have someone rescue them from their sin. Forgiveness is a choice, and these people have to make a choice to forgive themselves. They have to stop the behavioral patterns and habits of such sin and move on with their life.

Sexual sin knows no limits or boundaries. Sins of perversion cause people to lose their jobs, end their marriages and empty their bank accounts. People caught up in sexual sin have had to make lying a habit to cover up their addiction. They have to manipulate situations and be sneaky, so as not to get caught in their sin. Their justification is often, *Well, everyone is tempted by lust!* That is not true and is, in fact, a lie from the pit of hell. We all suffer temptation, but our temptations are different.

Ways lust enters your life

Lust brings on shame. We are not always responsible, however, for the key entry point in our lives behind the manifestation of lustful tendencies. Sometimes circumstances such as these open a door:

- Being a victim of sexual abuse
- Being exposed to extreme sexual circumstances
- Being forced to watch or participate in sexual activities
- Having sexual experiments and encounters with siblings or friends as a child
- Being attacked by demonic sexual spirits in the night, while in bed

Sexual spirits draw and lure you into the wrong way of thinking and acting. Seducing spirits lure you into thinking about and acting on the very thing you should not. It is a strong pull on your thoughts in a sexual direction. You have to fight hard in your flesh to defeat this pull. It requires conquering your thoughts and resisting temptation. You need to rise up and not only fight in the spiritual realm, but also fight in the natural.

You have to resist. If you don't, temptation is going to pull you constantly in the wrong direction, and you will never win the battle. You can't blame everything on a demon. You have to resist the temptation to give in to the demon luring you, because when you don't resist, you are co-laboring with the demon and giving it a legal right to manifest in your life.

Sexual or inappropriate visions

Sexual visions can tempt us while in church, in simple conversation or in moments when we are not even thinking lustful things. The enemy attacks us and disrupts our normal activities, including our worship time, by seducing us into lustful thoughts and visions. If he can plague our mind with these thoughts at inappropriate times throughout the day, he can penetrate our emotions to make us feel filthy and unworthy. The spirits that randomly and quickly attack us in this area are low-grade sexual spirits that we can cast out easily ourselves. Just say with authority, "Go, in Jesus' name," in a firm, audible voice.

Sexual abuse

If you are struggling to be delivered from a sexual spirit, spend time discovering whether there is Freemasonry in your generational line. If the sexual spirits resist expelling, they may be coming from a mason in your family line, especially from a grandfather. What was your relationship with your grandfather? Discovering the root of a sexual addiction will assist you in effectively casting out the strongman. People with strong sexual spirits that entered due to Freemasonry could have been sexually abused as infants or children by their grandfather or his friends, yet they don't remember it. Strongholds from this time period need to be broken. Vows and oaths from Freemasonry that are attached to these sexual spirits must be renounced, and the spirits cast out.

The majority of people I deliver don't remember their sexual abuse experiences, but they have had questions in the back of their minds about certain instances that happened in their lives. They just never took the time to get to the root and never gained the discernment or received revelation about these situations so that it could lead to healing. People often stuff their feelings and ignore what happened in the past. Here are some reasons people may not remember their abuse:

- They were given drugs.
- They were under alcoholic influence.
- They blocked the memory.
- They refuse to deal with the instance.
- They were taught to stuff their feelings.
- They are in denial.
- They were too young.

As we grow closer to the Lord, He will begin to reveal things in our past from which we need deliverance.

Dormant and slumbering spirits

Sexual spirits that gained entry through experiences people don't remember are dormant and slumbering spirits that need to be brought to the forefront and cast out. Even though we don't remember our abuse, it very much affects who we are today. The specifics of a sexual violation do not have to be remembered. We don't have to envision Jesus being in the situation.

What we need is to be delivered from the spirits and soul ties attached to these spirits. When we have been sexually abused and have not received the freedom Christ has for us, it holds us back from our full potential. We need to be set free from things in our past, whether or not we acknowledge that they are present in us.

Dormant and slumbering spirits affect our lives, ruin our destinies, keep us in bondage and steal our joy. These spirits begin to manifest as we grow closer to the Holy Spirit. Did you ever feel as though you were almost delivered, and *boom*, something manifested? Then you think, *Where did that come from?* The closer we get to the Holy Spirit, the more He purges us from hidden and forgotten strongholds. I have experienced this in my life and have been part of delivering many people of such dormant and slumbering spirits.

Issues we are unaware of affect who we are today. Spirit-filled, tongue-talking Christians can be and are in bondage. We are being held back from our full potential by issues in the past that have never been dealt with or by demonic spirits that have not been cast out. We are in bondage, and often we don't even know it.

Meditate on whether you can pinpoint a time where you were living in victory, walking a great walk with the Lord, and then you were again dealing with an issue you thought you had already dealt with or had victory over. Obviously, when you formerly dealt with the issue, behavioral pattern or habit, the demonic spirit associated with it was not cast out, or else you may have opened the door to sin and it entered back in. Now, years later, you are dealing with the same issue. If you cannot get complete freedom in an area of your life, dig deeper into your spiritual roots, your past, your parents' past, generational curses and soul ties. Find out about what is in your past, repent and renounce it, break agreement with it and command it to go. Root that thing out so you can be free now and in the future.

Healing from adulterous acts

Healing from adultery is twofold. You are either the person who has committed adultery, or you are the person hurt from your spouse committing adultery. Whatever position you are in, you need healing. You either have deep regret, guilt and remorse from committing adultery, or you have bitterness, resentment and deep hurt from an adulterous act committed against you.

Christ forgave us at the cross of all our sins. Healing and reconciliation start with us extending the same forgiveness to others that Jesus extended to us. We simply forgive because we choose not to allow unforgiveness to hold us in bondage anymore, and we want to accept and receive the finished atonement of the cross. You can talk all day about what happened and seek a counselor, but ultimately, the greatest thing everyone needs to do is forgive and extend Jesus' forgiveness to others (and themselves), as the Bible instructs.

Give yourself permission to grieve the loss caused by adultery in a marriage. Holding in the emotions surrounding what happened will not heal you; it will hurt you in the long run. Allow yourself to go through the normal process of grief and loss. Give the situation to the Holy Spirit and allow the healing balm of Jesus to come in and wipe away every tear.

The most difficult thing to do is forgive yourself. When you don't forgive yourself, you are keeping yourself in captivity. Feelings of guilt, condemnation, shame and regret must be removed. You need to grieve the situation and loss you created. But you cannot stay stuck in the guilt of your sin and the pain of your mistakes. You need to find a way to forgive yourself and move on. Forgiving yourself does not mean forgetting, but it is the first step toward healing.

Close the doors to the temptation of adultery in the future by talking to your spouse and working out your differences. If there is something that needs to change in your marriage, find a unified way to set goals and perimeters in place to overcome the challenges. Don't give up. Keep loving and have faith. Marriage is a covenant not only with your spouse, but with God. Through Him, all things are possible. Believe God for the impossible and for the healing that can happen.

Discerning the people to forgive

We need to discern the people we need to forgive in the areas of sexual abuse and addictions. I want to be very specific in this healing process so that we close all entry points and doors open to the enemy. Unforgiveness can lead to open doors the enemy can use to attempt to infiltrate our soul. The Bible instructs us not to be in bondage again (see Galatians 5:1), which means bondage can reenter. Please think about everyone and anyone you may have to forgive in order to pull out the strongman of unforgiveness and move on with your life to find full deliverance from anything related to lust. The following list of people to forgive covers this entire section on perversion, so make use of whatever applies specifically to your situation.

- Forgive your abuser.
- Forgive your parents if they did not stop the abuse or did not believe you when you confided in them about it.
- Forgive yourself, if applicable. Victims may feel as if they were partially to blame because of something they did or did not do.
- Ask God for forgiveness if, indeed, you had something to do with the situation; this could have been through flirtation, manipulation, drugs or alcohol.
- Forgive your sexual partner.
- Forgive your spouse if something he or she said or did could have pushed you away or could have been the reason you adulterously sought after another person.
- Forgive your offender if anyone forced you sexually or took advantage of you if you were on drugs or alcohol.
- Seek the Lord's forgiveness.
- Seek your spouse's forgiveness if he or she is aware of what took place and if you are being led by the Spirit.

Spend time in prayer and meditation, and seek the Holy Spirit about whoever was involved in your situation, whom you now need to forgive. Also note that I am not suggesting you run to your spouse and instantly confess your sin of adultery because of reading this. I do believe adultery should be confessed, but in the Holy Spirit's timing and not in a moment of guilt and flesh. I have seen many marriages remain intact if the confession is done in the leading and timing of the Holy Spirit.

Walking Out Your Deliverance

Walking out your deliverance in the area of sexual addictions and perversion will take accountability. Find someone of the same gender as yourself and ask that person to be your accountability partner. Reach out via text, email or a phone call whenever you are being tempted and feel led to participate in an unclean act, and expose the enemy by asking that person to pray for you.

Scriptures on Removing Sin

Psalm 51:2, 10; Ezekiel 36:25; John 15:3; 1 Corinthians 6:11; Galatians 5:15–16; Ephesians 4:22–32; 1 John 1:9

Prayer of Repentance and Forgiveness

Pray this prayer audibly to repent and release forgiveness:

Heavenly Father, I know I have participated in unclean acts, unclean thoughts and lust, which are against the Word of God. Please remove these desires from me. Fill the void I feel in my life, and heal the hurt in my past that led to these things. I know I do not have to be dependent on them. Forgive my generational line for the sin of lust and perversion that has come down to me. Forgive me so that I don't pass it along to my children. I forgive myself for participating in sexual desires that are against Your Word. Lord, help me forgive those who have committed adulterous acts or sexual defilement against me. I choose this day to release forgiveness toward those people and to accept the forgiveness Jesus gave me and others at the cross, in Jesus' name. Amen!

Spirits to Discern and Cast Out

Ask the Holy Spirit to reveal all the demonic spirits associated with sexual addictions and perversion that you need to cast out. Out loud, command these spirits to leave: "Spirit of _____, go, in Jesus' name!" You may have to do this several times over a period of time. Do it until you feel peace, a release or a spiritual shift. Spirits often associated with sexual addictions and perversion:

Adultery, anger, bitterness, blame, condemnation, foul, Freemasonry, generational curses, guilt, homosexuality, incest, lust, lust of the eyes, lust of the flesh, molestation, oaths, offense, pedophile, perversion, pornography, promiscuity, rape, regret, resentment, satanic ritual abuse, sexual abuse, torment, trauma, uncleanness, unforgiveness, ungodly soul ties, violation, vows

Prayer of Activation

Father God, I thank You that You have set a guard around my eyes and ears. Help me return to You in purity, love and devotion. I do not need the things of the world, or the lust and satisfaction of the flesh. I choose You, not unclean things and acts. I choose to live my life dedicated to You. I receive Your love, Your cleansing and Your wholeness deep down to the depths of my soul. I declare that I have a sound mind that thinks right thoughts. I believe I will walk in Your ways, Lord, moving forward, in Jesus' name. Amen!

Declarations to Speak Out

Speak out the following faith declarations and spiritual warfare declarations. Bookmark these pages and come back to them as often as necessary to assist you in renewing your mind, transforming your heart and increasing your faith.

Faith Declarations

Make these faith declarations audibly, with power and authority, believing that you will receive them. Speak them out from a position of *I have these*, not *I'm trying to obtain these*. While you transition from sexual addictions to healing and freedom, read these declarations out regularly to help you grow strong in faith and renew your mind.

- I declare and decree that I am free from lustful and perverse thoughts and actions.
- I keep myself and my ways before the Lord at all times.
- When temptation comes, I will not give in to old ways, habits, thoughts and patterns.
- My eyes are set on right things; my thoughts think right thoughts. I am moving forward, not backward.
- I receive instruction and conviction from the Lord and embrace them and activate on them.
- The Word of God is alive and active in me. I live out the Word of God in abundance.
- I will not be shaken or moved, because my feet are firmly planted on the foundation of Jesus Christ.
- I declare that my inner being is renewed day by day, in Jesus' name.

Spiritual Warfare Declarations

Make these spiritual warfare declarations audibly, with power and authority. When you speak out these declarations, you are taking up your God-given authority to bind and restrict the enemy and counteract future attacks. Declare them repeatedly, until you feel something release in the spiritual atmosphere.

- I diffuse every dark assignment coming against my path, leading me into temptation.
- I send disturbance into the enemy's camp, causing destruction and delay of his assignments against me.
- I bind and restrict every spirit of temptation or seduction, and luring spirits that try to draw me into sin. I rebuke you and your powers over me and command you to cease your assignment, in Jesus' name.
- I rescind every demonic order written against my destiny. I declare and decree I will not lose my job, marriage or anything else as a result of being lured into perversion.

- I speak and declare there will be no retribution from the enemy for my freedom. I will walk in my full purpose and destiny.
- I abort every perverse assignment in operation against me. You will not prevail.
- Every familiar spirit, cycle, season and pattern, I bind you; I restrict you. I command you to depart from my life, my home, my ministry and my workplace. You will not create the same negative cycles in my life.
- Every spirit of perversion and lust, be removed. Get out of my life now, in Jesus' name!

CLOSING PROPHETIC WORD

You have come to a new crossroad in your life. A new season, and a new reason for living. I have trusted you with the very things close to My heart. Now it is time for you to release what I have given you. You may have gone through a deep breakthrough, or you may be just at the beginning of the deliverance process. Remember, deliverance is a process. It is a constant mind renewal; it is a constant battle, but one I know you can fight and win. We have exposed the enemy and his tactics; now it is time to put on your battle artillery and fight and go to the next level. Your next assignment is spiritual advancement, regrowth and new opportunities. I have set a wide, effectual open door in front of you. Choose wisely, choose diligently. I have more in store for you.

Kathy DeGraw is a prophetic spiritual warfare and deliverance minister who releases the love and power of God to ignite and activate people, release their prophetic destinies and deliver them from the bondage of the enemy. Founder and president of Kathy DeGraw Ministries, Kathy is passionate about empowering people to serve and love God and others. She travels internationally and also brings her Be Love Prophetic Tours around the U.S., ministering through street evangelism and empowering believers to release the prophetic and "be love."

Kathy writes weekly for *Charisma Online* magazine and hosts the weekly *Prophetic Spiritual Warfare* show on the Charisma Podcast Network. She is a recognized prophetic voice on the Elijah List and in *Prophecy Investigators* online magazine. Author of books like *Speak Out*, *Discerning and Destroying the Works of Satan*, *Warfare Declarations*, *A Worship-Woven Life* and *The Sky's the Limit*, Kathy has also written a four-day deliverance school and three-day inner healing school in which she empowers churches and ministries to start their own healing and freedom ministry. Likewise passionate about bridging the divide of racism through her corporation Change Into Colorless, Kathy desires to bring forth healing, unity and love around the world through educating people on forgiveness and racial issues.

Kathy is married to Ron DeGraw, and together they co-pastor Ruach Ha'Kodesh Apostolic Empowerment Center. She is mom to three adult children, Dillon, Amber, and Lauren; they reside in Grandville, Michigan.

To inquire about hosting Kathy for a ministry event, contact
Kathy DeGraw Ministries
P.O. Box 65
Grandville, MI 49468
www.kathydegrawministries.org
admin@degrawministries.org